THE OPEN UNIVERSITY

Arts : A Third Level Course
Twentieth Century Poetry

Units 4-5

MODERNISM AND ITS ORIGINS

Prepared by P. N. Furbank and Arnold Kettle for the Course Team

The Open University Press

Cover Henri Gaudier-Brzeska, Bird swallowing a fish *c.* 1914 (Tate Gallery)

The Open University Press
Walton Hall   Milton Keynes
MK7 6AA

First published 1975. Reprinted 1977(with corrections)

Designed by the Media Development Group of The Open University.

Printed in Great Britain by
EYRE AND SPOTTISWOODE LIMITED
AT GROSVENOR PRESS PORTSMOUTH

ISBN 0 335 05102 2

This text forms part of an Open University course. The complete list of units in the course appears at the end of this text.

For general availability of supporting material referred to in this text please write to: Open University Educational Enterprises Limited, 12 Cofferidge Close, Stony Stratford, Milton Keynes, MK11 1BY, Great Britain.

Further information on Open University courses may be obtained from the Admissions Office, The Open University, P.O. Box 48, Walton Hall, Milton Keynes, MK7 6AB.

1.2

CONTENTS   UNITS 4-5

PART 1   P. N. FURBANK

1	Introduction	5
2	Imagism	7
3	*Symbolisme*	13
4	The 'Modernist' Attitude	25
5	'Modernism' and Tradition	30
6	Free Verse, the Prose-poem, and the Prose of Fiction	33
7	Obscurity in 'Modernist' Verse	41
8	Was 'Modernism' a good thing?	45
9	'Modernism' and the War	45

PART 2   ARNOLD KETTLE

1	The War Poets	49
	References	67

Figure 1   Rock Drill (1913–14) by Jacob Epstein (Tate Gallery)

MODERNISM AND ITS ORIGINS PART 1

1 INTRODUCTION

1.1 As you will have gathered, there was a major revolution in English verse just before the 1914–18 war, which is now generally called by the name of 'modernism'. It is a name to be used with caution, as it can be rather misleading. In the first place, it was not used at the time, but was coined much later by scholars. Pound did not call himself a 'modernist'. He called himself an Imagist, and later, for a time, a Vorticist. As for Eliot, he did not call himself by the name of any new movement; though later on, to the amazement of some of his followers, he declared himself a classicist in literature, a royalist in politics and an Anglo-Catholic in religion. Secondly, 'modernist' does not mean the same as 'modern'. The implication of the word, as I shall use it here, is that the movement is now over and may be seen as part of history. Thirdly, the name, of course, does not apply only to poetry. If we are to use the term at all, we must bear in mind that there was 'modernism' in prose fiction, and in music, and in painting, sculpture and architecture. If Pound and Eliot were 'modernists', then so, certainly, were Stravinsky and Schönberg, Picasso and Brancusi. Some scholars speak of 'modernism' in philosophy, theology and psychology, and even in mathematics and physics. And here we come up against a danger in the word. It is too convenient, you can always fall back on it when you do not mean anything in particular.

1.2 What is indisputably true is that there was an extraordinary outburst of intellectual and artistic activity in the early 1900s. It was one of the great periods in Western culture, and, further, it was an age of discovery. Everywhere the emphasis was on the *new*; *Make it New* was the title Ezra Pound gave to a volume of his essays, and it might have been the slogan for the age. New movements, new trends, followed one another with bewildering rapidity. The whole foundations of thought and knowledge seemed to be – and indeed were – shifting. One can make other simple generalizations. One can say that culture in this period was peculiarly cosmopolitan: Paris was aware of Vienna, and Vienna of St Petersburg, in a way that has not been true in many periods of history. It was also peculiarly eclectic. Artists felt themselves the inheritors of all past ages and of all parts of the globe, and free to make use of them and pillage them as they wished. Stravinsky flirted with Russian folk music, with Viennese eighteenth-century music, with Bach and with African tribal music. Ezra Pound donned the mask of a Provençal troubadour, a Latin poet of the Empire, and a classical Chinese lyrist.

1.3 It does not follow at all from this, though, that what was occurring was one movement – that there was something called 'modernism' trying to break out, like dry rot, all over the place. That is to give the word too definite a meaning; we would do better to go to the other extreme and define 'modernism' simply as 'all the new thought developing round about 1900–10'.

1.4 I think, though, there was more to it than that. For one thing, 'modernist' artists and thinkers were intensely aware of one another's work. Painters, in particular, sometimes collaborated very closely; Picasso and Braque, who invented Cubism in 1908 or thereabouts, sometimes could hardly remember later which of them had painted a particular canvas. Likewise, it often happened that a painter would try to achieve in painting the same thing as a poet whom he admired, and vice versa. I choose these as clear and specific examples of interrelation between 'modernists'. Beyond them spreads out a web of innumerable links, influences and cross-currents, both conscious and unconscious, between the artists and thinkers of the time, and we shall follow certain threads of this web in the present unit.

1.5　This still does not mean that there was something called 'modernism', if one means by that a definite movement with a definite set of doctrines. And for this reason I shall not, myself, offer a definition of 'modernism', for I think that more would be lost than gained by it. Let us think a little further about what sort of term 'modernism' is. It is not a term like 'Marxism' or 'Impressionism', which can be quite easily defined. It is not even a term like 'Conservatism'. For, though there are many conflicting definitions of Conservatism, there must come a moment, if you use the word at all, when you have to define it. A Tory candidate would look very foolish if he said he was sorry, but he couldn't quite define Conservatism, 'though of course he knew what it was'. A term that resembles 'modernism' more closely, I suggest, is 'the Renaissance'. Everyone defines the Renaissance differently; they even date it differently, by as much as a century. Nevertheless, it is a useful term, and means somewhat more than just 'Leonardo da Vinci, the Medici, Shakespeare and Machiavelli'. In the pages that follow I shall be talking confidently about the 'modernist' view of this and that, so in reading them you should remember these doubts and provisos.

1.6　Coming then to English poetry: which were the first poems in English to which we might apply the term 'modernist'? My list would be as follows. Certain poems written in 1908 and thereafter by what came to be known as the Imagist school of poets. Various early poems by T. S. Eliot, especially 'The Love Song of J. Alfred Prufrock', written in 1910–11 and first published in periodicals in 1915. D. H. Lawrence's sequence of free verse poems, *Look! We Have Come Through!*, published in 1917. And – since the midwife of 'modernism' in English verse was Ezra Pound – it seems right to include the two volumes, by no means his first, in which he attained maturity as a poet: I mean *Cathay* (1915) and *Homage to Sextus Propertius* (1917).

1.7　Viewing it in this way, we have a movement which began nearly a decade before the First World War and which does not appear to have been greatly deflected by the war. But also a movement which came rather late in Britain. Much had been happening already in literature in Paris and Vienna; and indeed important things had been happening in Britain, if one thinks of prose fiction. By 1908 Joyce had made, or was making, profound innovations in fictional technique. Prose fiction was in advance of poetry generally in Britain at this time: Henry James and Conrad had reflected more deeply on their art and made stricter artistic rules for themselves than any contemporary poets. And it became a favourite theme of Ezra Pound's that poets needed to learn from the prose writers – above all from Flaubert.

1.8　I have mentioned the First World War and said that, overwhelming event though it was, it does not seem to have altered the direction of 'modernism' fundamentally. What is equally true, however, is that the experience of trench warfare revolutionized the life and work of certain poets of a more traditional kind, notably Wilfred Owen, and caused them to write a quite new kind of poetry – new not only to themselves but to English literature. There are those who feel that Wilfred Owen's war poetry is more valuable and important than the poetry of Eliot and Pound and the other 'modernists'. However, it is convenient to treat it as something separate from 'modernism', and that is what we shall do in this unit. The first part of the unit will deal with 'modernism' proper, and the second (prepared by Arnold Kettle) will deal with Wilfred Owen and other war poets.

2 IMAGISM

2.1 Let me begin, then, with those Imagist poets of the immediate pre-war period. The Imagist movement may be said to have had its birth in a dining-club founded in London in 1909 by the poet and philosopher T. E. Hulme and another, now rather forgotten, poet, F. S. Flint. The history of the movement has been summarized very clearly by John Press, in his *A Map of Modern English Verse* (pp 30–6), and instead of my repeating the story here, the simplest thing will be to ask you now to read his account.

2.2 Just to test your grasp of these pages in John Press, you might like to ask yourself, and write down, what were the circumstances of the *naming* of the Imagist movement.

2.3 As you will have gathered from John Press, the prime tenet of the movement was the need for 'absolutely accurate presentation and no verbiage'. I will quote two poems from this period by T. E. Hulme:

> The lark crawls on the cloud
> Like a flea on a white body.

> *Autumn*
>
> A touch of cold in the Autumn night –
> I walked abroad,
> And saw the ruddy moon lean over a hedge
> Like a red-faced farmer.
> I did not stop to speak, but nodded,
> And round about were the wistful stars
> With white faces like town children.

■ How far do these measure up to the demands for 'absolutely accurate presentation' and 'no verbiage'?

Discussion

2.4 I think one can fairly pass them on the test of 'no verbiage'. Maybe the first poem will hardly seem to you a poem at all; just a jotting. But at all events, the second one gains its effects with notable economy. It presents what it wants to present in the fewest possible number of words, and then simply stops. It lies on the page like a seashell or a carving, and we are to make what we like of it.

2.5 What about 'absolutely accurate presentation', however? Well, in the first poem, 'The lark crawls on the cloud' certainly strikes one as very accurate and original; to have noticed that a hovering lark, against a cloud as background, seems to 'crawl', is evidence of a trained and unprejudiced eye. So perhaps does 'Like a flea on a white body', but 'absolutely accurate presentation' does not seem to me the most important thing here. The true *raison d'être* of this line, I suggest, is to imply: 'I am not tied down, like some late-Victorian poet, to sentimental clichés about larks and clouds and nature generally. If my eye tells me that a lark looks like a flea, I shall say so.' The same is true of 'Autumn', is it not? The poet is refusing to gush about nature and takes a cheerful, insouciant attitude towards it. Much of the point of the poem lies here, rather than in any special 'accuracy' of presentation; though its two main similes, likening the moon to the red face of a farmer and the stars to white-faced town children, are certainly very original, and appealing in an unexpected way. Pound called similes and metaphors the poet's 'pigment', in which he was trying to find a common ground for poets and painters; and, in general, we shall find that Imagist poems tend to centre upon a simile, though in Pound's case, unlike Hulme's, it is often not introduced by the words 'like' or 'as'. ■

2.6 Let us turn to another Imagist poem, this time one by Ezra Pound.

> *Fan-piece, for her Imperial Lord*
>
> O fan of white silk,
>   clear as frost on the grass-blade,
> You also are laid aside.

Is this a poem at all? What does it say? What is it about? Is it a description, and if so, to what point? I will do my best to answer these questions. If the poem evokes any feeling in you at all at a first reading, it may be nothing more precise than 'fragility' or 'delicacy'; but if it does so much as this, I would like you to ponder on how it comes to do so. What is there to cling on to? Well, first, I think, a contrast between the inanimate and the living: the white of the silk fan is plainly such a fresh, 'living' white that this inanimate thing puts one in mind of living and evanescent things, like frost and grass. But, next, if the poem itself seems so fragile, so insubstantial, could there not be a simple reason for this – that Pound wants it to *resemble* a delicate Chinese fan? We remember that a classical Chinese poem might actually be written on silk, in exquisite calligraphy, so that a poem and a fan would not be such very diverse things. But then, what is one to make of that last line, 'You also are laid aside' – for the whole poem, such as it is, seems to lead up to this line. What does it mean? The thing to do, in a case like this, is to let the line lie in one's mind, without trying to *force* a meaning from it, till suggestions and implications dawn.

2.7 Certain things are clear: the woman speaking has a fellow feeling for her fan. This inanimate object symbolizes for her something evanescent in her own life, which has to be renounced or resigned. But what that is, we may not be able to guess with certainty; though it will be something which a fan *would*, naturally, symbolize – something to do with the life of a high-born lady or fashionable courtesan. My own first guess at the sense was that a bride has to give up modesty (hiding her face with a fan); in making, or painting, a fan for her husband, or 'Imperial Lord', she is, as it were, making him a present of her modesty or virginity. This makes a beautiful poem, I think, but, as it turns out, not the right one! For I find that the poem, or at least the Chinese original, is about a discarded mistress, who is to be 'laid aside' or 'put on the shelf' by her 'lord' or noble lover (so she will no longer have occasion to ply her fan or exercise her attractions). I do not intend to feel too ashamed of my error, for I had enjoyed and loved the poem for years before I ever got down to working out the meaning of that last line, and the discovery does not fundamentally change the poem for me (though I think it does improve it). The lesson, perhaps, is how much of the real meaning of a poem of this kind lies as much in its *shape* as in its content. Every detail of its shape counts, and this is the justification of the doctrine: 'no verbiage'. This poem, especially in the way it culminates in that last line, resembles more than anything a gesture, a gesture performed with consummate grace – I might add, a gesture like the handling of a fan.

2.8 It is appropriate to have jumped from Hulme to Ezra Pound, for it was Pound who not only christened the movement but came to dominate it. Sometime in 1912 he and his fellow poets 'H. D.' (Hilda Doolittle) and Richard Aldington formulated three principles of *Imagism*:

a Direct treatment of the 'thing' whether subjective or objective.

b To use absolutely no word that does not contribute to the presentation.

8

c   As regarding rhythm: to compose in the sequence of the musical phrase, not in the
     sequence of a metronome.

Elsewhere, Pound gave his definition of an 'Image':

> An 'Image' is that which presents an intellectual and emotional complex
> in an instant of time . . . It is the presentation of such a 'complex' instan-
> taneously which gives that sense of sudden liberation; that sense of freedom
> from time limits and space limits, that sense of sudden growth, which we
> experience in the presence of the greatest works of art.

As you will see, Pound lays stress on the instantaneity of the 'Image'; it 'is that which
presents an intellectual and emotional complex *in an instant of time*'. What this reveals
is that Pound wants poetry to approach closer to painting and sculpture. Literature
is a time-bound art; you have to read the beginning before the middle, and the
middle before the end; it is a matter of one thing after another. Painting and sculpture,
on the other hand, are not time- or succession-bound. You can begin looking at a
painting or a sculpture where you like; and in a sense, it is possible to take in a painting or a sculpture at a single glance. Pound was deeply impressed by Post-Impres-
sionist painting and modern sculpture, and part of his motive in demanding 'use
absolutely no word that does not contribute to the presentation' was a yearning to
rival the plastic arts.

2.9 It was, after all, a very exciting moment in the history of the plastic arts, this of
     Picasso and Matisse and Brancusi and Gaudier-Brzeska. And thinking of poetry in
     this connection leads us on to a general characteristic of 'modernism' in the arts. One
     of its tenets was that art should be nothing but art; that is to say, it should not com-
     promise with entertainment, or instruction, or any other purpose extraneous to art.
     Even Impressionist painting, though considered in its time as very iconoclastic, does

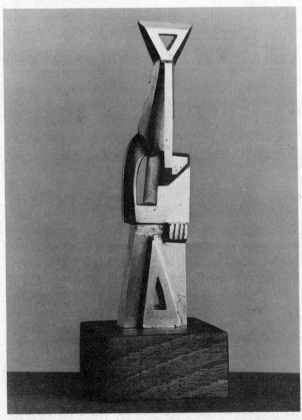

*Figure 2   Ornament/Toy by Henri Gaudier-Brzeska, discussed by Norbert
Lynton in the television programme 'Making It New' (Tate Gallery)*

not pass the 'modernist' test; for it continued to give the spectator various enjoyments which, in a strict view, were not intrinsic to art. An Impressionist landscape, for instance, gave him something of the same experience as he would receive from walking in the countryside. This seemed to the 'modernist' a kind of impurity. He felt that a painting or a poem need not be a copy of anything in nature. Natural objects and art objects were different and equal, and the artist was not the slave, but the rival, of nature or God.

2.10   We must now consider how this theory applies to poetry. At first there might seem to be a contradiction between asserting that a poem should not be a 'copy' of anything in nature, and the demand for 'direct treatment of the "thing" ', as prescribed by the Imagists. It is not really so, however. For, for one thing, Imagist poems work by comparing one thing with another. Let us take a poem by 'H. D.' (Hilda Doolittle)

> *Heat*
>
> O wind, rend open the heat,
> cut apart the heat,
> rend it to tatters.
>
> Fruit cannot drop
> through this thick air –
> fruit cannot fall into heat
> that presses up and blunts
> the points of pears
> and rounds the grapes.
>
> Cut the heat –
> plough through it,
> turning it on either side
> of your path.

This is certainly not a 'copy' of a heat-laden scene. I suppose you could say it was a copy of the poet's experience on such a day; but even this is not a very obvious way of describing it. For one thing, because the poem is full of imperatives, it is a plea or order to the wind to clear the stifling summer atmosphere. And for another, because it depends heavily on metaphor – on imagining the wind as a knife or chisel, and the heat-laden air as a solid body. Much of the strength of the poem lies in the energy with which these unlike things are held together in the poet's mind – and, indeed, it is a notably energetic poem. Where 'direct treatment of the "thing" ' comes in, is in the poet's refusing to explain the larger emotional or intellectual meaning of the experience. She does not say, like Keats in his 'Ode to a Nightingale', 'My heart aches and a drowsy numbness pains/My sense . . . etc.' And, denying herself such explanations, she can do without complicated sentence structure; she can restrict herself to urgent, bare imperatives. She can create the illusion that the poem stands there, impersonal, like a material object.

2.11   This point, that an Imagist poem works by comparing one thing with another, without further comment, has some importance, though it is not stressed in the Imagist manifestoes. Its significance will be plain if we consider another poem of 'H. D.'s':

> *Oread*
>
> Whirl up sea
> whirl your pointed pines,
> splash your great pines
> on our rocks,
> hurl your green over us,
> cover us with your pools of fir.

■ C. K. Stead, in his book *The New Poetic*, speaks of this poem as being about a forest, as compared with the sea. But could it be read, almost as well, as being about the sea, as compared with a forest? Try the experiment.

Discussion

2.12 I really think, myself, you could – at least if you ignored the title, which means 'mountain nymph' and so tips the balance towards forest. The fact tells you a good deal about Imagist poetry. For evidently, if you do not know whether someone is talking to you about fir trees or about the sea, he cannot, in the ordinary sense of the word, be making a statement about life, or indeed a 'statement' about anything. Now this marks a difference between Imagist poetry and most poetry one is familiar with. If you think of almost any poem by, say, Wordsworth or Tennyson or Thomas Hardy, you will see that it is making some statement, some direct comment on life. To take an example at random, Thomas Hardy's 'The Oxen' (p 91 in Creighton) says (I am paraphrasing brutally) that, though modern man cannot literally believe the country superstition that at midnight on Christmas Eve the cattle go down on their knees, nevertheless he may still poignantly wish to believe it. Now, however hard you look at 'Oread', you can squeeze no such statement about life out of it. The poet is saying 'Here is a perception or observation about the external world: I leave you to piece out its human meaning.' Of course, it has human meaning: the poem is an intuition about life; and if it is successful, if the perception is rendered accurately, the reader, by re-enacting the perception, will be enabled to share the intuition.■

2.13 Let us approach Imagism, finally, in another and easier way. Imagism is not merely a theory or a movement; it is also, for each of the Imagist poets, a style. One can recognize Pound's 'Imagist' style quite easily. Listen to these two poems of his:

April

   Nympharum membra disjecta[1]

Three spirits came to me
And drew me apart
To where the olive boughs
Lay stripped upon the ground:
Pale carnage beneath bright mist.

Gentildonna

She passed and left no quiver in the veins, who now
Moving among the trees, and clinging
                    in the air she severed,
Fanning the grass she walked on then, endures:
Grey olive leaves beneath a rain-cold sky.

The last lines, so similar in their construction, are very characteristic of Pound's 'Imagist' style. Having set up a scene or event, full of complex suggestiveness, he clinches the experience in a line which simply sets one object beside another: 'Pale carnage beneath bright mist', 'Grey olive leaves beneath a rain-cold sky.' This particular trick of style remained with Pound long after he ceased to call himself an Imagist, and is thus a minor legacy of Imagism.

[1](Latin) The scattered limbs of nymphs.

11

2.14 Pursuing this approach, let us consider a more important legacy of Imagism. One of the striking things about 'H.D.'s' poem 'Heat' is its hesitant, impeded motion, hardly moving forward at all, as if there were great gulfs of air or silence round each word or phrase. Now read this, from Eliot's *The Waste Land* (1922).

> The river sweats
> Oil and tar
> The barges drift
> With the turning tide
> Red sails
> Wide
> To leeward, swing on the heavy spar.
> The barges wash
> Drifting logs
> Down Greenwich reach
> Past the Isle of Dogs.

Isn't the movement of it very similar? It seems so similar to me, that I would guess that Eliot definitely learned from 'H.D.' Though there are differences too: Eliot's lines have a song-like quality, and indeed in its context the passage is meant to be a song. And another interesting point arises here. For if I am right that Imagist poems almost always, and on principle, centre upon some comparison, simile or metaphor – seas being like fir trees, the wind behaving like a knife or chisel etc. – then Eliot is not writing an Imagist poem here; for the lines contain no simile, nor likening of this thing to that, at all. I surmise that one reason why the Imagist movement was short-lived, was that this habit or principle of centring your poem on a comparison proved, in the long run, rather constricting. Pound seems to have found it so, and moved on beyond it, as 'H.D.' attempted to, though with less success.

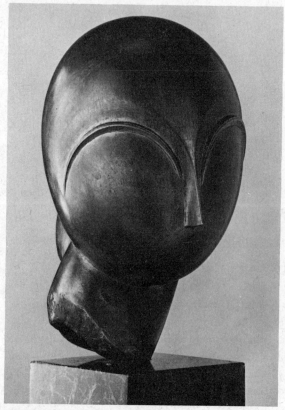

Figure 3 Danaide c. 1913 by Constantin Brancusi (Tate Gallery © A.D.A.G.P. 1975)

2.15 Here is a poem from a later period which I think it would be not unreasonable to call 'Imagist'. (It is by the American poet William Carlos Williams and was first published in the 1930s.) As you will see, it contains no metaphors or comparisons at all.

Poem

As the cat
climbed over
the top of

the jam closet
first the right
forefoot

carefully
then the hind
stepped down

into the pit of
the empty
flowerpot

■ Do you see why I call it 'Imagist'?

Discussion

2.16 For the reason that it simply 'presents' something, an action, without any sort of commentary, or indeed without any sort of hint of the kind of feeling it is meant to evoke. Surely a very 'impersonal' poem in the Pound sense!

2.17 It is a poem which may not 'come off' for you. However I like it myself, for all that it seems so devoid of almost all the things that one expects in poetry: no obvious 'point', no appeal to the emotions, nothing at all interesting in the language. All the strength of the poem lies, I suggest, in its *movement*, which perfectly renders a mind taking in first one thing then another thing. The poem convinces me that the poet has looked at this cat with the whole of his being – as if, like Adam, he were seeing such a thing for the very first time.■

3 SYMBOLISME

3.1 Even in its heyday, Imagism was far from being the only concern of Ezra Pound. By 1913 he had become the focus and propagandist for 'modernist' writing and ideas in general. He had taken his friend Yeats in hand and was doing his best to 'modernize' him. ('He [Pound] . . . helps me to get back to the definite and concrete and away from modern abstractions', Yeats wrote to his friend Lady Gregory; 'to talk over a poem with him is like getting you to put a sentence into dialect. All becomes clear and natural.') He also planned to do the same for Robert Frost – who, however, prudently or cravenly, fled the country. He had discovered Joyce and was going to extraordinary lengths to encourage him and get his work published. And, finally, early in 1914, he discovered Eliot, a poet who, he found, had 'modernized' himself independently; and he began a similar campaign of propaganda on his behalf.

3.2 Now, Eliot and Yeats had developed, in their own individual ways, from a tradition very different from that of Imagism. Their roots were in *Symbolisme* – that poetic school of the 1880s in France, the leader of which was Stéphane Mallarmé, and which included Verlaine, Rimbaud, Tristan Corbière and Jules Laforgue.

3.3 In discussing *Symbolisme* I shall have to go back to these French poets of the 1880s, and so to a period thirty years before 'modernism' proper. However, before doing so, I would like to offer a rather crude but helpful distinction. There may be said to be two streams in 'modernist' verse writing, one which took its inspiration from words, and one which took its inspiration from things. The Imagists belonged to this second stream. They were turned outwards towards the external world. For them, the great enemy was 'abstraction'. Virtue for a poet, in their view, lay in attending to 'things', and they would have liked their poems to have had the solidity and substance of 'things'. This remained the ambition of Pound, long after he had left Imagism behind; and 'No ideas but in things', a slogan coined by William Carlos Williams (1883–1963), is a belief still influential in poetry, especially American poetry, today.

3.4 The *Symbolistes*, by contrast, put their faith in words. You might say of them that they wished for no further contact with the world than is provided by the dictionary. This is not as absurd as it sounds, considering that we do our thinking in words. Of course, any poet needs a stimulus from something outside him, otherwise he would not write; but the *Symboliste* poet tends to take his stimulus from words themselves. The poet, according to Mallarmé, 'surrenders the initiative' to words and finds much of his inspiration in the accidents and fortuitous 'marriages' of words. His ultimate ambition is to replace the universe as we know it by a self-sufficient universe of words.

3.5 Let me try, then, briefly to give an historical sketch of the *Symboliste* movement. It is not too easy a task. First, because the *Symboliste* poets were very different from one another, and though they agreed in calling themselves by the name *Symboliste*, they explained the term in very diverse – not to say confusing – ways. And secondly, because the acknowledged leader of the movement, Stéphane Mallarmé, is a rather difficult and obscure poet. Thus, there are two temptations to be resisted: to think that by prolonged meditation on the word *Symbolisme* we can finally arrive at a comprehensive definition, which will cover and explain everything the *Symbolistes* wrote; or, going to the other extreme, to conclude there was no such thing as a *Symboliste* movement – only a group of poets who thought they were engaged in a common endeavour but were mistaken. Two other approaches will prove more fruitful. The first is the historical one: that is to say, to consider certain doctrines which were much discussed among the circle, regardless of whether they hang together as a whole, or, indeed, whether we can altogether make sense of them. The second is what you might call an *ad hoc* or empirical one: I mean, to consider the poems of Mallarmé and draw what conclusions we can from them. We will be on firm ground in this latter, for no one can dispute that, if there is such a thing as *Symboliste* poems, then that is what Mallarmé's are. They are poems unlike any previously written; some of them, at least, most critics would agree, are extraordinarily beautiful and impressive, though very rarefied, elusive, and, to some tastes, 'precious'; and they had a strong influence on later poets.

3.6 To follow up the first of our approaches, then. One leading notion among *Symbolistes*, is that there is an inner reality to the world, of which the things that we perceive by our eyes and ears are merely a symbol, and to which poetry enables us to penetrate. The poet thus becomes a kind of seer or mystic. Taken to extremes, the theory holds that any concrete thing is a 'symbol', and that there is a secret system of 'correspondences' between the objects of our five senses, so that certain sounds are inseparably linked to certain colours and to certain odours and so on. Viewing poetry in this manner, the poet, in looking at the external world is searching for a combination of objects which will correspond to some inner state of feeling; this is his only interest in the outer world. Mere things, mere objects, do not interest him for their own sake, and much of the art of poetry will lie, for him, in suggesting objects without precisely naming them. Here is how Mallarmé puts it:

> To name an object outright is to destroy three-quarters of the enjoyment of
> a poem, which depends on a gradual process of guessing; to *suggest*, that
> is the ideal. It is perfect skill in this art which constitutes the *symbol*: evoking
> an object little by little in order to show forth a state of the soul.

3.7 There follows from this attitude an implication about the poet's role. His function is an other-worldly and contemplative one. He need not, and should not, concern himself with social, political or moral problems. The *Symboliste* movement was a movement of revolt against the positivist and materialist tendencies of nineteenth-century life and of mid-nineteenth-century theories of art and literature: it rejected the theory that art and literature should serve social good and deal with human problems in a 'scientific' and rationalist manner. As a consequence, *Symboliste* poetry tends to strike a note of ethereality, world-weariness and quietism. The *Symbolistes* shunned rhetoric, which is the language of those who want to influence and dominate their fellow men. (Verlaine wanted to 'wring rhetoric's neck'.) They shunned moreover all purposeful, bustling, rhythmic energy – such as you find in Robert Browning, say – and cultivated instead a subtle, uncertain, broken-backed rhythm, as of men who have renounced the will.

3.8 Here is how Yeats describes the *Symboliste* ambition:

> With this change of substance, this return to imagination, this understanding
> that the laws of art, which are the hidden laws of the world, can alone
> bind the imagination, would come a change of style, and we should cast
> out of serious poetry those energetic rhythms, as of a man running, which
> are the invention of the will with its eyes always on something to be done
> or undone; and we would seek out those wavering, meditative, organic
> rhythms, which are the embodiment of the imagination, that neither desires
> nor hates, because it has done with time, and only wishes to gaze upon
> some reality, some beauty . . . ('The Symbolism of Poetry', 1900. Reprinted
> in the Course Reader.)[2]

3.9 We should notice that, in their attitude to society, the *Symbolistes* had gone a step further than the Romantic poets. The Romantics, like them, attacked what they regarded as the soulless rationality of their age, and, in order to do battle with it,

[2]Graham Martin and P. N. Furbank (eds.) (1975) *Twentieth Century Poetry: Critical Essays and Documents*, The Open University Press.

they were ready to embrace isolation. Nevertheless, they *did* do battle. They preached and exhorted, or cast themselves in the role of Prometheus, who stole fire from Heaven on mankind's behalf, and, though chained to a rock in punishment by Zeus, still glared defiance at his conqueror. By contrast, the *Symbolistes* renounced the will and all striving and accepted isolation without complaint. They washed their hands of society. Of course, this too was a way of doing battle with it.

3.10   Yeats, who began writing in the 1880s, was much under the influence of the *Symbolistes*, and a very early poem, 'The Song of the Happy Shepherd', might be called a *Symboliste* manifesto. Here is the second of its three sections:

> Then nowise worship dusty deeds,
> Nor seek, for this also sooth,
> To hunger fiercely after truth,
> Lest all thy toiling only breeds
> New dreams, new dreams; there is no truth
> Saving in thine own heart. Seek, then,
> No learning from the starry men,
> Who follow with the optic glass
> The whirling ways of stars that pass –
> Seek, then, for this is also sooth,
> No words of theirs – the cold star-bane
> Has cloven and rent their hearts in twain,
> And dead is all their human truth.
> Go gather by the humming sea
> Some twisted, echo-harbouring shell,
> And to its lips thy story tell,
> And they thy comforters will be,
> Rewording in melodious guile
> Thy fretful words a little while,
> Till they shall singing fade in ruth
> And die a pearly brotherhood;
> For words alone are certain good:
> Sing, then, for this is also sooth.

Another poem of his belonging to this period illustrates very memorably the 'unworldly' note of *Symbolisme*.

> ### The Indian to his Love
>
> The island dreams under the dawn
> And great boughs drop tranquillity;
> The peahens dance on a smooth lawn,
> A parrot sways upon a tree,
> Raging at his own image in the enamelled sea.
>
> Here we will moor our lonely ship
> And wander ever with woven hands,
> Murmuring softly lip to lip
> Along the grass, along the sands,
> Murmuring how far away are the unquiet lands:
>
> How we alone of mortals are
> Hid under quiet boughs apart,
> While our love grows an Indian star,
> A meteor of the burning heart,
> One with the tide that gleams, the wings that gleam and dart,

The heavy boughs, the burnished dove
That moans and sighs a hundred days:
How when we die our shades will rove,
When eve has hushed the feathered ways,
With vapoury footsole by the water's drowsy blaze.

It is, I think you will agree, a marvellously beautiful poem, achieving in that last line an extraordinary synthesis of conflicting impressions: tenuousness and fervency, shadowiness and definition. The kind of living it celebrates, however, is the most twilit, ethereal affair imaginable, altogether a kind of death-in-life: far away indeed are ethics or effort or any active concerns. You may say that it is just 'escapist' poetry, a weak kind of dreaming such as has earned Victorian poetry a bad name; but I think you would be wrong. For is there not a vigour and challenge in its very renunciation of the busy striving world? The energies of the world have been stilled but not extinguished; indeed the poem is full of these energies – the parrot 'rages', the Indian's love, though twilit, is to burn like a meteor. What we have in this poem, I suggest, is not escapism at all, but an impassioned ascetic contemplativeness, not very different from what Yeats will express much later in his 'Byzantium' poems. There is a difference, however. The poem is very hushed and rapt, quite unlike the robustness and ribaldry of the later Yeats, and he has learnt this note from the *Symbolistes*. So far as Yeats is concerned, the phrase in use was the 'Celtic twilight', this being a local version of the *Symboliste* tradition. What we have in the young Yeats is something very characteristic of the period: the spectacle of very vigorous, combative, rather worldly men writing deliberately limp and 'unworldly' poems.

3.11   I have cheated a little over 'The Indian to his Love', for what I have given is Yeats's final version of the poem. The first version, written some thirty years earlier (it was published in 1886), runs as follows:

An Indian Song

Oh wanderer in the southern weather,
    Our isle awaits us; on each lea
The pea-hens dance, in crimson feather
    A parrot swaying on a tree
    Rages at his own image in the enamelled sea.

There dreamy Time lets fall his sickle
    And Life the sandals of her fleetness,
And sleek young Joy is no more fickle,
    And Love is kindly and deceitless,
    And life is over save the murmur and the sweetness

There we will moor our lonely ship
    And wander ever with woven hands,
Murmuring softly, lip to lip,
    Along the grass, along the sands –
    Murmuring how far away are all earth's feverish lands:

How we alone of mortals are
    Hid in the earth's most hidden part,
While grows our love an Indian star,
    A meteor of the burning heart,
    One with the waves that softly round us laugh and dart,

Like swarming bees; one with the dove
    That moans and sighs a hundred days;
– How when we die our shades will rove,
    Dropping at eve in coral bays,
    A vapoury footfall on the ocean's sleepy blaze.

3.12 I think you will agree that the later version is strikingly superior, and though the differences are not exactly my concern here, you might like to ponder them fairly carefully and ask yourself what they consist in and why they are improvements. It is a comparison that reveals a good deal about Yeats's development, and something about the development of English poetry in general in the twentieth century. I am not going to insist on 'modernist' influence, but one can imagine the yelp of rage with which Pound would have greeted those flabby personifications 'dreamy Time', 'sleek young Joy', for example.

POETRY AS MUSIC

3.13 Another doctrine most *Symbolistes* were agreed upon was that poetry should approach as close as possible to music. There are really two quite distinct ideas here: the idea that poets should cultivate the 'music' of verse – the subtle harmony and delicate assonances and dissonances of vowels and consonants; and the idea that poetry should emulate the purity of music, its power to express, quite directly, states of the soul and of feeling.

3.14 As regards the first sense, certain of the *Symbolistes* – especially Verlaine and Mallarmé – did very assiduously cultivate 'music' in their verse, so that the first feature that strikes one in some poems is not the meaning, but words combined in cunning, subtle and novel harmonies. It is not easy to illustrate the kind of 'music' from English poets, because of the great difference between French and English versification. So here, for those who read French, is a famous poem by Verlaine which aims almost wholly at 'music'.

> Il pleure dans mon coeur
> Comme il pleut sur la ville;
> Quelle est cette langueur
> Qui pénètre mon coeur?
>
> Ô bruit doux de la pluie
> Par terre et sur les toits!
> Pour un coeur qui s'ennuie
> Ô le chant de la pluie!
>
> Il pleure sans raison
> Dans ce coeur qui s'écoeure.
> Quoi! nulle trahison?
> Ce deuil est sans raison.
>
> C'est bien la pire peine
> De ne savoir pourquoi,
> Sans amour et sans haine,
> Mon coeur a tant de peine!

You can perhaps form a faint impression of what Verlaine is attempting from a poem by Ernest Dowson (1867–1900), who was a follower of Verlaine. It will only be a faint impression, because the 'music' is much more obvious and less subtle.

Exile

> By the sad waters of separation
>   Where we have wandered by divers ways,
> I have but the shadow and imitation
>   Of the old memorial days.

In music I have no consolation,
    No roses are pale enough for me;
The sound of the waters of separation
    Surpasseth roses and melody.

By the sad waters of separation
    Dimly I hear from an hidden place
The sigh of mine ancient adoration:
    Hardly can I remember your face.

If you be dead no proclamation
    Sprang to me over the waste, grey sea:
Living, the waters of separation
    Sever for ever your soul from me.

No man knoweth our desolation;
    Memory pales of the old delight;
While the sad waters of separation
    Bear us on to the ultimate night.

■ What is your general reaction to this poem? How would you answer a critic who found it too 'poetic' altogether; who objected to Dowson's solemn and lugubrious posturing and his antiquated vocabulary ('The sigh of mine ancient adoration' etc.); who, indeed, thought it an empty poem, doing no more than say, in embroidered language, 'It is so long since we parted that I can hardly remember what you look like, and this makes me very sad'? Could you level the same criticism at it as Graham Martin (rightly, to my mind) levels at Robert Bridges' 'A Passer-By', in Unit 1 (3.6 and 3.7)?

Discussion

3.15 Personally, though I have envisaged all these objections, I like Dowson's poem. I find it haunting, for all that it has such a 'dated' air (somehow, the word 'dated' seems apt here, though it is not a word one would normally apply to poetry). The 'music', which is so insistent – the plangent chiming of those reiterated sounds and syllables and cadences: 'Sever for ever your soul from me', and so on – seems genuinely beautiful and poignant to me. I would defend the poem against the Robert Bridges one by saying that, unlike Bridges, Dowson does not pretend to be saying very much. His attention is focused upon 'music' – a particular music, crepuscular and defunctive, which does, truly, succeed in expressing a mood. (It was almost the only mood that Dowson, a very minor poet, ever learned to express.)■

3.16 A word about 'music' may be in place here, to prevent misunderstanding. An ear for the physical properties of words is a faculty absolutely essential to any good poet, and its scope goes far beyond 'music'. No poet possessed a more developed 'ear' than Shakespeare – I mean, a sense for all the various ways in which the mere physical act of pronouncing vowels and consonants in sequence can be made to evoke and embody meaning. Think of such lines as these from *Measure for Measure*:

    Ay, but to die, and go we know not where;
    To lie in cold obstruction and to rot;
    This sensible warm motion to become
    A kneaded clod; and the delighted spirit
    To bathe in fiery floods, or to reside
    In thrilling region of thick-ribbèd ice;

Never did verse express with such power, as that last line, a man shuddering to the depths of his being; and this is achieved, in part, through a sort of physical mimicry of a man shuddering, embodied in the very way the line has to be pronounced. Shakespeare, however, is not aiming at 'music' here, but something quite different. Elsewhere, in the songs in his plays, he does sometimes aim at 'music'; and it is interesting to note that the *Symbolistes* particularly admired Shakespeare's songs.

3.17 The second sense of 'music', perhaps more important, would take me too far from my subject, which is not so much *Symbolisme* itself as *Symbolisme's* contribution to the 'modernist' movement.

DISTRUST OF 'IDEAS'

3.18 A further idea important to the *Symbolistes*, and to Mallarmé in particular, is that 'ideas' themselves, in the everyday sense of the word, are alien to poetry. Earlier nineteenth-century poetry, both in France and Britain, tended to be full of ideas: political ideas, religious ideas, ideas such as one might write out in prose and argue about and make the subject of a book or an essay. It was part of the *Symbolistes'* disengagement from contemporary life that they came to distrust ideas in this sense. (A poem such as Housman's 'Others, I am not the first', discussed in Unit 1, 3.12, would have seemed to Mallarmé too explicitly *about* something, too easily paraphrasable.) Mallarmé did not banish 'ideas' from his theory of poetry, but he gave the word a special, mystical and transcendental meaning. As A. G. Lehmann puts it, in his *The Symbolist Aesthetic in France*, ideas for Mallarmé 'are not confined to the realm of the intelligible, or rather intellectual, speech, but may be found in any form of art, and especially ballet . . . and we are led to the conclusion that for the poet, poetry and art is something very much wider than the communication of opinions – it is symbolic gesture in the widest sense: the expression of attitude'. Mallarmé wanted poetry to emulate not only music but the dance. He would speak, for instance, of a dancer's legs as 'a direct instrument of ideas'. Part of the point of this is a claim for the self-sufficiency of art and poetry. A solo dance can be very 'expressive' without being *about* anything or referring to anything outside itself, and Mallarmé would have liked the same to be true of a poem. Its 'form' and its 'content' should be the same thing.

3.19 It is a complex and elusive theory, but an important one, not only for the *Symbolistes* but for their successors, and we shall have to grapple with it more fully in the units on Eliot and Yeats. Meanwhile, I will just quote a passage from Yeats's 'Among School Children', written in the 1920s, the last two lines of which seem like an echo of Mallarmé's theory:

> Labour is blossoming or dancing where
> The body is not bruised to pleasure soul,
> Nor beauty born out of its own despair,
> Nor blear-eyed wisdom out of midnight oil.
> O chestnut-tree, great-rooted blossomer,
> Are you the leaf, the blossom or the bole?
> O body swayed to music, O brightening glance,
> How can we know the dancer from the dance?

You should look up the whole poem in *Collected Poems of W. B. Yeats*, but I shall not discuss it here, merely having wanted to bring evidence of Mallarmé's enduring influence. (If you are interested, you will find a long discussion in Frank Kermode's *Romantic Image* (1957).)

THE LONG POEM

3.20 A problem of special difficulty for the *Symboliste* poet, and one which Mallarmé wrestled with throughout his career, was how to compose a long poem. Long poems in the past have had a principle of continuity which lay outside them. Virgil's *Aeneid* spoke for the whole Roman civilization and Empire; Dante's *Divine Comedy* spoke for medieval Catholicism. But a *Symboliste* poem, according to the strictest theory, though it has to be prompted by something outside the poet, is not exactly *about* that thing – it is not *about* anything at all, but self-sufficient and self-justifying. And on this basis, it is hard to see what a *Symboliste* can do, having written one poem, but to write another different one. It is difficult to see how he can construct an extended work.

3.21 Mallarmé, nevertheless, was not satisfied with this, and throughout his life he wrestled with the idea of a long work, one which would be quite different in nature from his short poems. It was to be 'architectural and premeditated, not a collection of chance inspirations, however marvellous'. As the years passed, extraordinary rumours circulated about this projected masterpiece; that (to quote A. G. Lehmann) 'it was to be in twenty volumes, that it was esoteric in the extreme, that it was to be typographically disposed for the uninitiated to read it without cutting the pages, etc.' It never got written, and Mallarmé, though he sometimes encouraged the rumours, would in more rueful moments refer to it as 'the Monster-which-cannot-be'. We shall see that the 'modernist' poets inherited this problem.

MALLARMÉ AND LANGUAGE

3.22 We will now proceed to our second approach to the movement, via Mallarmé's actual poems. An important truth comes home to us as soon as we do. What Mallarmé's poems, as opposed to his theories, reveal is that the true novelty of *Symbolisme* lies in a wholly new attitude to language. As theorists, the *Symbolistes*, even Mallarmé, were handicapped by an inadequate notion of language. The current notion, from which even Mallarmé did not quite escape, was that language was a set of arbitrary tokens, by means of which – as by coins – poetic conceptions were exchanged between poet and reader. The poet composed a poem in his head and then looked about for the right words by which to communicate it. This made the turning-into-words of a poem a purely mechanical affair; and since the *Symbolistes* sensed, none the less, a great mystery in poetry, they fell back on the explanation that the poet was a seer, channelling arcane knowledge to the reader, like a mystic or a prophet. (Hence the theories I have discussed under 'Mystical *symbolisme*'.) The truth, as a later generation of poets and critics have seen it, is that the mystery lies in language itself. The poem does not exist until the poet begins to write it; and perhaps not even then, for – this is a common experience – he may write words that at first he does not himself understand but which, as it were, attract a meaning to themselves when written. Using language, in any manner, is a creative act; it is by language that we construct the world for ourselves. (You will remember Graham Martin's discussion of this in the television programme *Language and Imagery*.) For a poet, using language is also an act of discovery. In writing a poem the poet is, you might say, bringing to light something that has lain concealed in the language since the dawn of time.

3.23 Extravagant language, you may think. But Mallarmé's poems show him to have held just these views. He was more aware of the nature of words than any previous poets, and he took much of his inspiration from words themselves. He perceived, moreover, that words – by which I also mean grammar and syntax, and even typographical layout – could be made expressive in ways other than those we are accustomed to in normal speech. He twisted language into strange forms, so that if you are expecting normal rational statements from his poems, you will be frustrated. Sentence constructions in his poems are sometimes no more than the husks or shells of normal statements or constructions; they work on us in another way from the normal one. It is difficult to illustrate this in translation. I will quote one attempt at translation from Mallarmé, by Roger Fry, but only to emphasize that he is untranslatable.

Victoriously Fled

Victoriously fled is the grand suicide
Glow of glory, blood in foam, tempest and gold.
Ah, ha! if down there a purple is spread
To pall royally my absence of tomb.

What! of all that splendour not even a shred
Lingers on, it is midnight, in our festival shade
Except that presumptuous treasure of head
Which pours without torch its languor caressed,

Yours! so ever delightful, ah yours!
Which alone of the sky that is vanished retains
What with puerile triumph you wind in your hair

Shining when on your cushion it lies
Like the warrior casque of an empress child
Whence, to figure yourself roses should pour.

The original, of which the translation only manages to convey the oddity, not the beauty, runs as follows:

Victorieusement fui le suicide beau
Tison de gloire, sang par écume, or, tempête!
Ô rire si là-bas une poupre s'apprête
À ne tendre royal que mon absent tombeau.

Quoi! de tout cet éclat pas même le lambeau
S'attarde, il est minuit, à l'ombre qui nous fête
Excepté qu'un trésor présomptueux de tête
Verse son caressé nonchaloir sans flambeau,

La tienne si toujours le délice! la tienne
Oui seule qui du ciel évanoui retienne
Un peu de puéril triomphe en t'en coiffant

Avec clarté quand sur les coussins tu la poses
Comme un casque guerrier d'impératrice enfant
Dont pour te figurer il tomberait des roses.

But whether one is reading the translation or the original, one point is clear: the meaning and the value of the poem do not lie in its statements.

3.24 We shall do better if we fall back on an English poem; and, once more, a poem by Yeats.

Who goes with Fergus?

Who will go drive with Fergus now,
And pierce the deep wood's woven shade,
And dance upon the level shore?
Young man, lift up your russet brow,
And lift your tender eyelids, maid,
And brood on hopes and fear no more.

And no more turn aside and brood
Upon love's bitter mystery;
For Fergus rules the brazen cars,
And rules the shadows of the wood,
And the white breast of the dim sea
And all dishevelled wandering stars.

◼ What do you feel about this poem? What sense do you make of the question it opens with ('Who will go drive with Fergus now') or of the statements it makes ('For Fergus rules the brazen cars')? If you do not make much sense of them, does this matter? Can you guess who Fergus is, or, if not, should the fact trouble you? Can you find another word in the poem which seems to be linked in meaning to 'woven' in the second line? And if you are bored with these questions, but like the poem (as I do, very greatly), can you define at all what it 'says' to you? Or are you content to fall back on some such epithet as 'magical', or 'evocative'?

Discussion

3.25 I think that one can fairly call this a *Symboliste* poem. To me, at least, it conveys not just a vague 'magic' but a very definite meaning, though I should be hard put to it to put the meaning in other words; and that is just what one should expect of a *Symboliste* poem. I have no idea who Fergus is, further than that he is a figure in Irish mythology and, presumably, a demigod, or hero with supernatural powers. It would be quite easy to look him up, but all the better, I feel, if I can get on without this: I might find out too much, or the wrong thing. Certain matters seem clear, none the less. Fergus, and driving with Fergus, signifies vigour and briskness and discipline, as opposed to introspection and Romantic disorder. The point of my question about 'woven' was that a contrast seems to be made between the orderly 'woven' shade of the wood, which is Fergus's domain, and the 'dishevelled' stars, which require him to keep them in order. This is a piece of mythologizing which it needs no knowledge of Celtic lore to attach a meaning to: most of us, at some time or other, have told ourselves to 'brace' ourselves, to stop brooding and turn our energies outwards.

3.26 However, this most certainly is not an adequate paraphrase. To take just one objection: it does not help us to understand the question 'Who will go drive with Fergus now?' This is not exactly an invitation (like 'Who's for tennis?') or exactly a demand for information. It is deliberately ambiguous. Yeats is not necessarily saying that going with Fergus is a good thing. It could be – there is a faint suggestion of this in those 'brazen cars' – that the Fergus way of living is a ruthless, unfeeling, even you might say fascist, affair. We never receive an answer to that opening question, 'Who . . . ?' It is like a corridor which leads nowhere. And I offer this as a tiny example (there are others in the poem) of what I was saying about Mallarmé: his sentence constructions being only the husks or shells of normal sentence-constructions. ◼

3.27 Another example might be the following passage from Eliot's *The Waste Land*, which is a poem much influenced by *Symbolisme*.

Here is no water but only rock
Rock and no water and the sandy road
The road winding above among the mountains
Which are mountains of rock without water
If there were water we should stop and drink
Amongst the rock one cannot stop and think
Sweat is dry and feet are in the sand
If there were only water amongst the rock
Dead mountain mouth of carious teeth that cannot spit
Here one can neither stand nor lie nor sit
There is not even silence in the mountains
But dry sterile thunder without rain
There is not even solitude in the mountains
But red sullen faces sneer and snarl
From doors of mudcracked houses.

As you will see, the passage is full of half-completed sentences which turn back upon themselves or slide unexpectedly into other sentences, a process accentuated by the absence of all punctuation. (Eliot's intention in the passage is to evoke a dream-like situation or dilemma from which the speaker cannot escape.)

Figure 4   Red Blue Chair (1914) by Gerrit Rietveld; Norbert Lynton discusses a Rietveld chair in the television programme 'Making It New' (Victoria and Albert Museum)

24

4 THE 'MODERNIST' ATTITUDE

4.1 I have used Yeats to illustrate one feature of *Symbolisme*, its other-worldliness. However, Yeats's version of *Symbolisme*, by the 1900s, was somewhat out of date, as was English poetry in general. A point one should remember is that, as the British Empire expanded in the century's closing years, so, culturally speaking, did Britain withdraw from Europe. 'In the last decade of Victoria's reign', says Samuel Hynes in *The Edwardian Turn of Mind* (1967), p 308, 'one could not buy a translation of Zola's *La Terre*, or Dostoevsky's *The Idiot* or *The Possessed* or *The Brothers Karamasov* in London, or see a public performance of Ibsen's *Ghosts*, or look at any pictures by a French Impressionist in any gallery, either public or private. The new thought of Europe had been kept out of England, as though by quarantine.' The quarantine affected *Symboliste* poetry. *Symbolisme*, in the English mind, was associated with absinthe and 'decadence'. It is true that Ernest Dowson had produced a few fine translations of Verlaine; and it is true also that Oscar Wilde and George Moore had proclaimed the importance of the *Symbolistes*. However, Wilde, at least, hardly understood them; and the scandal of his own trial in 1895 confirmed the British public in its worst suspicions about *Symboliste* 'decadence'. The scandal set going a cult of 'healthiness' and Philistinism in English verse – a trend typified by Henry Newbolt. The publication of Arthur Symons's *The Symbolist Movement in Literature* in 1899 did a little in the way of spreading understanding, but the book reached a very small audience.

4.2 Thus, a prime need of the British writer in the early 1900s, if he took his art seriously, was simply to educate himself, to catch up with developments of twenty years earlier in France and other European countries. Joyce conducted such a self-education, round about the turn of the century, thereby becoming more than a home grown Irish writer. Eliot did so too, and the reading of Arthur Symons's book round about 1908 was a turning point in his development. And Ezra Pound becomes significant here. Pound, a tireless though wildly unsystematic self-educator, had also a passion for educating others. (Gertrude Stein, the American *avant-garde* novelist, called Pound a 'village explainer', adding that, not being a village, she did not feel the need of him.) As I have said, one of Pound's enterprises was to take Yeats in hand, at the elder poet's invitation, in order that he might 'modernize' him; and the result of this 'modernization' – however much or little it actually owed to Pound – was that more of the everyday man got into Yeats's poems. He shed that part of *Symbolisme* which had proved constricting to him.

4.3 Another need of the writer and artist was to fortify his independence. Given the stagnant condition of official English culture, and the spread of cheap fiction and mass circulation dailies, a writer with high ambitions could hardly hope to be popular, as his predecessors had been. He might, to begin with at least, have to write mainly for his fellow writers, a tiny audience indeed; and to face this fact and not let it daunt him called for much toughness. The writers of the English 1890s had faced it in their own way, a tragic way. They made a tragic drama of their relations with the public, resorting to absinthe or 'diabolism' or taking refuge in Catholicism (though perhaps 'taking refuge' is not a fair way of putting it). Living out their poetry in their lives, in this way, they quickly burned themselves out, ending up in alcoholic wards or as suicides. There may have been integrity in this, but in the long run it was bad for poetry, for poetry requires a back-breaking labour. We may recall Yeats's lines in 'Adam's Curse':

A line will take us hours maybe;
Yet if it does not seem a moment's thought,
Our stitching and unstitching has been naught.
Better go down upon your marrow-bones
And scrub a kitchen pavement, or break stones
Like an old pauper, in all kinds of weather;
For to articulate sweet sounds together
Is to work harder than all these, and yet
Be thought an idler by the noisy set
Of bankers, schoolmasters, and clergymen
The martyrs call the world.

Thus, a poet needs to keep in physical training, and to husband his resources.

4.4 The *avant-garde* writers and artists of the new century took the lesson, and what we see in them is the development of a tougher, more resilient, more cheerful and intransigent attitude towards society. What they wanted, above all, was to *work*, to be allowed to produce – and by hook or by crook they set themselves to secure the minimum conditions for this. They presented themselves to the world, and to themselves, as artificers, with tools and equipment kept in good working order. They cultivated not a suffering but a buoyant attitude towards society – teasing it, bullying it, or strewing bombs under its feet, according to their temperament. I am generalizing wildly, again, but this is not an altogether false picture of the public stance of Joyce and Eliot, as of Picasso and Stravinsky and many others of the *avant-garde* of the time.

4.5 Now, Pound, when he appeared on the London scene in 1908, was a supreme example of this attitude. He was tirelessly energetic, indefatigably creative, a *poseur* and a pest, but someone who prized, above all, what he called the 'factive personality', the determination to *make* things. In a way, his art and his propaganda were one; he hammered at the stupidity of the British reading public with the same energy, if not the same precision, as he 'hammered' at poems or as a sculptor might hammer at marble. However, to believe, as he did, that art should be nothing but art, should contain no extraneous ingredients, is not the same as to believe in 'art for art's sake'. On the contrary, Pound believed strongly in the social value of art. He considered that artists braced and purified society by their example – by exhibiting self-discipline and by eschewing flabbiness, sentimentality and sloppiness of mind. Poets, in particular, had a social function, in his view, since they deal with words which are the natural bond of society. Thus, their duty was to defend the language and keep it in good order. Eliot came to take a rather similar viewpoint. And T. E. Hulme was to push the identification between 'order' in poetry and 'order' in society to a point verging on fascism.

4.6 We should not think that 'modernism' means getting rid of *Symbolisme*. Pound, it is true, disliked *Symbolisme*. He associated it with 'mushy technique'. And, more importantly, it was antipathetic to him in its attitude to the external world. For him, the visible world was the source of all value and truth. To use and to discipline the eye was for him the supreme human activity; and thus the attitude of the *Symboliste*, who regarded the visible world as an illusion, a mere assemblage of symbols of an other-worldly reality, seemed to him arrogant and impious. But if Pound disliked *Symbolisme*, Eliot was steeped in it. And indeed it is in Eliot that the full potentialities of *Symbolisme* were at last realized in English verse. 'The Love Song of J. Alfred Prufrock', whatever else it is – and it is rather unplaceable – is a *Symboliste* poem.

4.7 We can thus take Pound and Eliot as our representatives, respectively, of the cult of things and the cult of words (see 3.3). This oversimplifies very greatly, for I do not at all mean that the Pound school was not interested in words and language. Quite the contrary. One of the differences between Pound and the Georgians was that Pound

Figure 5 Housing at Pessac, Bordeaux by Le Corbusier 1925) (F. R. Yerbury. Courtesy of Miss M. Morrison)

had a stricter and more resourceful feeling for language and insisted that every word in a poem must justify itself – there must be no slack, secondhand, 'fill-up' words or phrases. (Graham Martin comments: 'It was a sort of Leninism of literature – "Words that don't work won't eat".') I mean, rather, that Pound did not share the feeling of the *Symbolistes* that words were the be-all and end-all of poetry and that the discoveries that the poet made were not discoveries about the external world but rather discoveries about the potentialities of language. Perhaps I can make the point plain by quoting a *Symboliste*, or at least *Symboliste*-influenced, poem by the American poet Wallace Stevens.

Banal Sojourn

Two wooden tubs of blue hydrangeas stand at the foot of the stone steps.
The sky is a blue gum streaked with rose. The trees are black.
The grackles crack their throats of bone in the smooth air.
Moisture and heat have swollen the garden into a slum of bloom.
Pardie! Summer is like a fat beast, sleepy in mildew,
Our old bane, green and bloated, serene, who cries,
'That bliss of stars, that princox of evening heaven!' reminding of seasons,
When radiance came running down, slim through the bareness.
And so it is one damns the green shade at the bottom of the land.
For who can care at the wigs despoiling the Satan ear?
And who does not seek the sky unfuzzed, soaring to the princox?
One has a malady, here, a malady. One feels a malady.

If one has tended to think of *Symboliste* poetry as solemn, this should remind us that it can be extravagant, show-off and light-hearted. But above all, surely, what one can sense from this poem is that the author is infatuated with words. Take the title, for a start: he has chosen those two words 'Banal' and 'Soujourn' not so much because they accurately described what the poem is about as because they marry together in a strange, delightful and evocative way. (And as I have said earlier, a strictly *Symboliste* poem – which this is not, though it is much influenced by *Symbolisme* – cannot properly be said to be 'about' anything.) As for the poem itself, the poet has,

27

it is true, responded, and responded intensely, to the external world: it is, surely, a marvellous rendering of a sun-laden, somnolent afternoon scene? But what interests him more than the visible scene is his own mood; and what interests him more than his mood is the adventures among words that this mood sets going. The words positively jostle for our attention – too much so, perhaps, when it comes to 'For who can care at the wigs despoiling the Satan ear?' Stevens has got carried away by his game with words, and it is probably not much good beating one's brains to find a definite meaning for this line: though I suppose 'wigs' may be short for 'earwigs' (as well as having its normal sense); summer is being likened to mankind's 'old bane' the devil, a sluggish Satanic monster; and the 'ear' that the 'wigs' are despoiling is an ear of corn – i.e. the harvest.

4.8   Thus I think my distinction between the cult of things and the cult of words has some value; and we need not worry too much at its being an over-simplification, for the reason that the cult of words and the cult of things are not so opposed to each other as they might sound. At least, their exponents found they had important beliefs in common. One was the simple but important belief that poetry should be intelligent. There is much to admire in the verse of, say, Walter de la Mare, but it is not, or not usually, what one could call intelligent. He plays the innocent; he pretends to be less intelligent than he is; and in this he is rather characteristic of the Georgians. The quality of mind displayed in Georgian poetry would look feeble if set beside that of contemporary science or philosophy. 'Modernist' writers, on the other hand, admitted no inferiority to other sorts of intellectual, and indeed made a fair claim to be more rigorous and profounder.

4.9   Another belief held in common was that distrust of 'ideas' which we have already encountered with the *Symbolistes*. This may sound like a contradiction of what I was saying about intelligence, but it is not so really. What it means is that 'modernist' poets regarded poetry as a way of thinking about the world different from but equal if not superior to that of science or philosophy or social thought. The poet, they held, 'thinks' in poetry, thinks very profoundly, but he does not do so by means of 'ideas'. A poem is not just a translation of ideas into rhythmical language; on the contrary, it is something richer than any 'idea' and a more efficient way of interpreting the world. The poet – according to the language sometimes used by Yeats and Pound – aimed to create an 'image'; a meaningful but untranslateable entity, at one and the same time an idea and a 'thing'.

4.10   A further shared belief was that good poetry is impersonal and works by indirect means. The poet is not a man speaking directly to a listener, offering him the spectacle of his personality and emotions. This was how the Romantic poet, or one type of Romantic poet – the Shelleyan kind – thought of himself; and the 'modernists' united in distrusting Romanticism. In their view, the poet should stand aloof from his poem. 'All that is personal soon rots', said Yeats; 'it must be packed in ice or salt'.[3] Here is how Eliot speaks of 'impersonality':

> . . . the poet has not a 'personality' to express, but a particular medium, which is only a medium and not a personality, in which impressions and experiences combine in peculiar and unexpected ways. Impressions and experiences which are important for the man may take no place in the poetry, and those which become important in the poetry may play quite a negligible part in the man, the personality. ('Tradition and the Individual Talent', 1919. Reprinted in the Course Reader.)

[3]'A General Introduction for my Work', 1919. Reprinted in the Course Reader.

4.11 According to this view, the poet should not try to evoke emotion directly, but should interpose something between himself and the reader, leaving it to this to evoke emotion. The poet should conceal or obliterate himself. He may do so by presenting objects without comment, as in Imagism. Or another way is by his donning a 'mask' or 'persona', a face not his own. Ezra Pound at different stages of his career adopted a whole series of 'masks' or impersonations, writing in the guise of a troubadour poet, or a classical Chinese lyrist, or a Roman elegist. He said in his *Gaudier-Brzeska* (1916):

> In the 'search for oneself', in the search for 'sincere self-expression', one gropes, one finds some seeming verity. One says 'I am this', that or the other, and with the words scarcely uttered one ceases to be that thing.
>
> I began this search for the real in a book called *Personae*,[4] casting off, as it were, complete masks of the self in each poem. I continued in a long series of translations, which were but more elaborate masks.

Yeats was equally obsessed with 'masks' and flirted with the idea that all happiness, all active virtue, depended upon the power to assume a face that was not one's own. He wrote in *Per Amica Silentia Lunae* (1918):

> I find in an old diary: 'I think all happiness depends on the energy to assume the mask of some other life, on a re-birth as something not one's self, something created in a moment and perpetually renewed; in playing a game like that of a child where one loses the infinite pain of self-realisation in a grotesque or solemn painted face put on that one may hide from the terror of judgement . . . Perhaps all the sins and energies of the world are but the world's flight from an infinite blinding beam'; and again at an earlier date: 'If we cannot imagine ourselves as different from what we are, and try to assume that second self, we cannot impose a discipline upon ourselves though we may accept one from others, and active virtue, as distinguished from the passive acceptance of a code, is therefore theatrical, consciously dramatic, the wearing of a mask.'

4.12 One can consider it as a sign that the 'modernist' period was coming to an end, that, in the 1950s, a number of poets, especially American ones, began to rebel against the doctrine of 'impersonality', and to write 'confessional' poetry: for instance Allen Ginsberg in *Howl* (1956), a poem which is a deliberate pouring-out of emotion, very bardic and Romantic in manner; or again Robert Lowell, in *Life Studies* (1959), in which he writes quite directly and simply (or apparently simply) about his own family and childhood.

[4]Pound collected his early poems under the title *Personae*.

5 'MODERNISM' AND TRADITION

5.1 We come now to another aspect of 'modernism' – its relationship to tradition. What we cannot help noticing about Pound and Eliot (and Joyce and Stravinsky and Picasso) is their extraordinary eclecticism. These artists raided the past without compunction, appropriating whatever appealed to them. Eliot, for instance, borrows phrases and whole lines from Dante and Baudelaire, Middleton and Longfellow. Contemporary reviewers sometimes called this plagiarism, but it was something quite different.

5.2 One explanation given by the writers themselves, as I have said, was that the poet needed a 'mask' or 'persona'. There is more to eclecticism than the putting-on of 'masks', however. Artists such as those I have mentioned felt themselves to be at the end of an epoch. Something had worn out, perhaps for ever, and that was the unspoken assumption that for each subject matter there was a 'natural' and traditional style; so that if, when writing a lyric, you sounded like Herrick, or when writing an impassioned soliloquy, you sounded like Shakespeare, this was because, in English, that was the natural way to write. Keats and Wordsworth still felt this confidence. Keats had no particular self-consciousness in writing at times, like Shakespeare, nor did Wordsworth in writing, at times – say, when composing a sonnet – like Milton.

5.3 Since their time, however, this easy relation to the past broke down for complex reasons of social history; and what we tend to feel, in reading the Georgian anthologies, is how eclectic, how derivative, in a bad sense, the poets are, falling into Shakespearianisms or Keatsianisms or Wordsworthianisms just as it suits them, whereas nowadays a relationship to the past is something which needs to be fought for.

5.4 As an example of what I am talking about, consider a poem by Edward Thomas.

October

The green elm with the one great bough of gold
Lets leaves into the grass slip, one by one, –
The short hill grass, the mushrooms small, milk-white,
Harebell and scabious and tormentil,
That blackberry and gorse, in dew and sun,
Bow down to; and the wind travels too light
To shake the fallen birch leaves from the fern;
The gossamers wander at their own will,
At heavier steps than birds' the squirrels scold.
The rich scene has grown fresh again and new
As Spring and to the touch is not more cool
Than it is warm to the gaze; and now I might
As happy be as earth is beautiful,
Were I some other or with earth could turn
In alternation of violet and rose,
Harebell and snowdrop, at their season due,
And gorse that has no time not be gay.
But if this be not happiness, – who knows?
Some day I shall think this a happy day,
And this mood by the name of melancholy
Shall no more blackened and obscurèd be.

Thomas can be a fine and original poet, but this particular poem, 'October', strikes me as derivative in a bad way – that is to say, the poet does not know how derivative he is being. It is a delicate and difficult matter, this question of a poem's being 'derivative'; for I am not in the least saying that a poet should never echo an earlier poet, which would be an absurd infringement of his rights. It may help to divide the question into two separate issues. A poet may imitate or echo the general style of a poet, or a school of poetry, of an earlier age; or he may echo actual, well-known lines from an earlier poet. As to the first, one can make no general rules about it, for it will depend entirely on the particular poet as to whether his dependence on earlier poetry is fruitful or parasitic. When it comes to the second, the echoing of actual lines, however, I think one can make one demand, which is that the poet should know that he is doing it and why. (In Part 2 of these units Arnold Kettle argues that Wilfred Owen quotes from Keats consciously and deliberately and to great effect. See Part 2, paras. 1.42–1.43.)

5.5 Now my impression of 'October' is that there are several well-known passages from Wordsworth and Keats lurking behind it.

>   the wind travels too light
>   To shake the fallen birch leaves from the fern;

faintly recalls Keats's lines in *Hyperion*, Book 1:

>   No stir of air was there,
>   Not so much life as on a summer's day
>   Robs not one light seed from the feather'd grass,
>   But where the dead leaf fell, there did it rest.

>   The gossamers wander at their own will,

brings to mind Wordsworth's line in his 'Sonnet Composed upon Westminster Bridge':

>   The river glideth at his own sweet will:

>   Were I some other or with earth could turn
>   In alternation of violet and rose . . .

reminds one of the last stanza of Wordsworth's 'A slumber did my spirit seal':

>   No motion has she now, no force;
>   She neither hears nor sees;
>   Rolled round in earth's diurnal course,
>   With rocks, and stones, and trees.

You may say that the resemblances are very slight and could easily be coincidental. On the other hand, these are all very famous passages from Keats and Wordsworth – just the sort of thing that Thomas, if he had been at all eager to avoid echoes, would have been alert to. The poem gives me the impression that Thomas's feelings on that October day were less a spontaneous response to the natural scene than a comfortable 'literary' reverie; and this is a kind of writing that the 'modernists' were impatient with.

5.6 The 'modernist' writers felt strongly on this matter of one's relationship to past literature. Their reaction, however, was not to throw tradition overboard, but to re-examine their relationship with it with scrupulousness and honesty. If you are going to borrow, they said to themselves, then don't pretend that you are not borrowing. Accordingly they borrowed openly, assiduously and enterprisingly; and in the process of this dressing up in borrowed clothes they inaugurated an age great both in translation and in 'imitation' – the greatest age for these since the time of Dryden.

5.7 Whether raiding the past has anything to do with 'tradition' is questionable, of course. One has to remember that Pound and Eliot were both Americans, and so unlikely champions of the European tradition. (Another American, the critic Yvor Winters, likened Pound to 'a barbarian in a museum'.) At all events, if it *was* tradition, these poets established a special, what you might call 'semi-detached', relationship to it. They were by no means its humble servants. Their behaviour here was the same as their behaviour in strict matters of craft, and especially in versification. Both Eliot and Pound were very great innovators in versification, and the nature of their innovation is suggested by a quotation from Eliot's 'Reflections on *Vers Libre*' (1917):

> . . . the most interesting [free] verse which has yet been written in our language has been done either by taking a very simple form, like the iambic pentameter, and constantly withdrawing from it, or taking no form at all and constantly approximating to a very simple one. It is this contrast between fixity and flux, this unperceived evasion of monotony, which is the very life of verse.

> We may therefore formulate as follows: the ghost of some simple metre should lurk behind the arras in even the 'free-est' verse; to advance menacingly as we doze, and withdraw as we rouse. Or, freedom is only freedom when it appears against the background of an artificial limitation. ('Reflections on *Vers Libre*'. Reprinted in the Course Reader.)

All good verse that is based on strict metre works by creating endless variations within that metre. Eliot's innovation is merely a logical extension of this. He wrote a kind of verse which 'approaches' and 'withdraws' from some traditional metre. Sometimes he withdraws so far that, for a moment, one is not sure what metre he is alluding to. Let us take an example from his *Ash Wednesday*:

> At the first turning of the third stair
> Was a slotted window bellied like the fig's fruit
> And beyond the hawthorn blossom and a pasture scene
> The broadbacked figure drest in blue and green
> Enchanted the maytime with an antique flute.

Only 'The broadbacked figure drest in blue and green' is indisputably an iambic pentameter, yet the exhilarating sense of freedom given by the passage, as of verse tugging at its moorings, comes from its being anchored by this line to the iambic mode.

5.8 This is what Eliot calls 'taking a very simple form, like the iambic pentameter, and constantly withdrawing from it'. The reverse procedure – 'taking no form at all and constantly approximating to a very simple one' – is what we more specifically think of as 'free verse' or *vers libre*, and I shall discuss this later (para. 6.7) in connection with D. H. Lawrence.

5.9 Just as they approached and withdrew from traditional metres, so did Eliot and Pound claim the right to approach and withdraw from tradition in general. This freedom was something which had to be paid for, however. For one thing, it made it difficult for them to write a long poem – indeed impossible in the manner in which long poems have been written in the past. For to compose a long poem it has always been thought essential to commit yourself to a 'style'; and *committing* themselves to a style – giving up the right to 'approach' and 'withdraw' from differing styles as it suited them – is just what the 'modernist' poets found impossible. A 'mask' is not the same as a 'style', and to compose a long poem in a mask, which everyone knows is not your true face, would obviously be a hopeless enterprise.

5.10 Here we have a central difficulty and challenge, which we have already seen the *Symbolistes* wrestling with (see 3.20–3.21). The 'modernist' poets gave some of their deepest thought to it, and the answer they arrived at was a radical one. It was that, in the modern age, a long poem could only be constructed out of short ones. It had to be a succession of self-sufficient poems, set side by side; and it must always remain a matter of doubt to what extent the 'long poem', as distinct from its components, really exists. It is really the old Imagist argument against 'abstraction'; there must be no abstract framework, no cement, whether of argument or narrative or explanation. The bricks or stones must simply be laid beside or upon one another. And just as a short poem, for an Imagist, is a bringing together of concrete particulars, so a long poem is a bringing together of short poems, interacting with one another, correcting each other by contrast, and throwing out feelers to one another, in virtue of their independence. As this course proceeds, we shall see how Yeats, Eliot and Pound, so different as poets, found themselves led to a somewhat similar conclusion on this issue.

6 FREE VERSE, THE PROSE-POEM AND THE PROSE OF FICTION

6.1 One of the important contributions of *Symbolisme* to 'modernism' was *vers libre* or 'free verse': verse, that is to say, which breaks the bonds of traditional versification. Free verse was not the invention of the *Symbolistes*; there was, for instance, the powerful example of Walt Whitman, whose *Leaves of Grass* (1855) is perhaps the most ambitious of all enterprises in free verse. Nevertheless it was the *Symbolistes* who worked out a theory or rationale for free verse, and their influence was long-lasting. Most 'Imagist' poetry was written in free verse; indeed it is hard to imagine it being written in traditional metre and rhyme. You will remember Pound's advice: 'As regarding rhythm: to compose in the sequence of the musical phrase, not in sequence of a metronome.' Much of Eliot's work is in free verse, and so is the most important work of D. H. Lawrence.

6.2 ■ I have already (para. 5.7) quoted Eliot's distinction about free verse: that there are two kinds of broad categories within it – verse which takes a traditional verse form, like the iambic pentameter, and continually withdraws from it, though never altogether severing contact with it; and verse which begins with no verse form at all but continually approaches or approximates to one. This seems very helpful; and before we go any further you might like to try an exercise. To which of the two categories do you consider the following poems to belong?

33

La Figlia Che Piange

O quam te memorem virgo . . .

Stand on the highest pavement of the stair –
Lean on a garden urn –
Weave, weave the sunlight in your hair –
Clasp your flowers to you with a pained surprise –
Fling them to the ground and turn
With a fugitive resentment in your eyes:
But weave, weave the sunlight in your hair.

So I would have had him leave,
So I would have had her stand and grieve,
So he would have left
As the soul leaves the body torn and bruised,
As the mind deserts the body it has used.
I should find
Some way incomparably light and deft,
Some way we both should understand,
Simple and faithless as a smile and shake of the hand.

She turned away, but with the autumn weather
Compelled my imagination many days,
Many days and many hours:
Her hair over her arms and her arms full of flowers.
And I wonder how they should have been together!
I should have lost a gesture and a pose.
Sometimes these cogitations still amaze
The troubled midnight and the noon's repose.

'And oh –
That the man I am
Might cease to be –'

No, now I wish the sunshine would stop,
and the white shining houses, and the gay red flowers on the balconies
and the bluish mountains beyond, would be crushed out
between two valves of darkness;
the darkness falling, the darkness rising, with muffled sound
obliterating everything.

I wish that whatever props up the walls of light
would fall, and darkness would come hurling heavily down,
and it would be thick black dark for ever.
Not sleep, which is grey with dreams,
nor death, which quivers with birth,
but heavy, sealing darkness, silence, all immovable.

What is sleep?
It goes over me, like a shadow over a hill,
but it does not alter me, nor help me.
And death would ache still, I am sure;
it would be lambent, uneasy.
I wish it would be completely dark everywhere,
inside me, and out, heavily dark
utterly.

Discussion

6.3 The first poem, which is in fact by Eliot, belongs, surely, to the first of his two categories? One feels it to be in a metre, to have a regular metrical music running through it, and one even feels one can name the metre – it is the iambic pentameter – though that metre is, concertina-like, distorted and stretched and compressed in innumerable ways, and only one line, the last, is a regular example of the metre. But anyway, the poem rhymes, which is a traditional factor. And though the rhymes do not fall regularly, we feel that the poem, nevertheless, has a rhyme *scheme*, though one might be hard put to it to say precisely what this scheme is. But note particularly the line:

> And I wonder how they should have been together!

It is a wonderfully 'free' line, as though that thought, or pang, had just this moment impinged on the writer's mind and had been expressed in the very first words that occurred to him. This is a device that Eliot learned from the *Symboliste* poet Jules Laforgue and one that he puts to very telling effect elsewhere too, especially in 'Prufrock'. It is one of the devices, though device is too pedantic a word, which justify the relative 'freedom' of this kind of free verse.

6.4 As for the second poem, it seems to me to belong very definitely in the second of Eliot's categories. Many of its lines sound metrical: for instance

> the darkness falling, the darkness rising, with muffled sound

or

> but heavy, sealing darkness, silence, all immovable.

One can imagine them occurring in a poem in traditional metre. Again, the lines

> Not sleep, which is grey with dreams,
> nor death, which quivers with birth

form a couplet which, one feels, might quite easily have occurred in a poem of very obvious, even thumped-out, rhythm – one by Swinburne, say. What one cannot imagine, however, is all these lines occurring in the *same* traditional poem. One has no sense of a foreordained metrical scheme, a regular metrical music, lurking, however well concealed, in the background. There is not the impression of a poet making preliminary rules for himself and then following them.

6.5 Would you then say that the poem was formless?

6.6 Hardly, I think. For it is no illusion when, for a moment, it seems to approach some traditional metre. This is not an accident which we are meant to ignore or turn a deaf ear to. Anyway, apart from metre, the lines surely seem, in fact, very highly organized. There is a high degree of control, and rhetorical timing, in the way the words 'dark' and 'darkness' are made to gather emphasis at each repetition. Freedom, evidently, is not the same thing as lack of organization. And when we reach that concluding one-word line, 'utterly', we feel – or at least I feel – a strong sense of a goal reached and reached unerringly. ∎

6.7 Nevertheless freedom, initial freedom, freedom from the foreordained, is, we feel, of the essence in verse of this kind. And the implication is that the poet is placing a special value on spontaneity. Free verse of this nature goes with a particular attitude towards the world, which places organization and order second to impulse. This, at all events, was the attitude of D. H. Lawrence – and as you may have guessed the poem is by Lawrence, from his remarkable sequence of poems *Look! We Have Come Through!* (1917). The sequence traces the inner history or rhythm, at a very deep level, of Lawrence's feelings during the first stages of his elopement with Frieda Weekley, with the 1914–18 war as counterpoint to this. And, as the title suggests, it leads up to the poet's conviction of having 'come through' to some obscure victory. Most of the poems, however, were written before this 'coming through', so the extent to which we feel the sequence has form and coherence must depend on the extent to which the human experience itself, in retrospect, seems to have had a hidden direction. Thus, you will see, the basic principle of the work is very close to the principle of free verse in general: that is to say, pattern and organization, but no *foreseen* pattern and organization. Lawrence explains his attitude to free verse in the Introduction to his *New Poems* (1918):

> To break the lovely form of metrical verse, and dish up the fragments as a new substance, called *vers libre*, this is what most of the free-versifiers accomplish. They do not know that free verse has its own *nature*, that it is neither star nor pearl, but instantaneous like plasm . . . It has no finish. It has no satisfying stability, satisfying for those who like the immutable. None of this. It is the instant; the quick.

He also said something else about *Look! We Have Come Through!*, in his prefatory Note to his *Collected Poems* (1928):

> It seems to me that no poetry, not even the best, should be judged as if it existed in the absolute, in the vacuum of the absolute. Even the best poetry, when it is at all personal, needs the penumbra of its own time and place and circumstance to make it full and whole. If we knew a little more of Shakespeare's self and circumstances how much more complete the Sonnets would be to us, how their strange, torn edges would be softened and merged into a whole body! So one would like to ask the reader of *Look! We Have Come Through!* to fill in the background of the poems, as far as possible, with the place, the time, the circumstance. What was uttered in the cruel spring of 1917 should not be dislocated and heard as if sounding out of the void.

It is a far cry from Eliot and his doctrine of impersonality and the self-sufficiency of the work of art! You will see why I am so chary of defining 'modernism'. For I want to call *Look! We Have Come Through!* a 'modernist' work, yet I do not want to have to resort to sophistry to do so.

6.8 We are not devoting a separate unit to Lawrence's verse in this course, and though I shall say one or two more things about it here, I shall be dealing with it less for its own sake than for what it reveals about free verse in general. This, I am afraid, is an injustice to Lawrence, whose verse is of extraordinary interest.

6.9 One of the further points I want to make with the aid of Lawrence, concerns the *sound* of verse. If you compare Lawrence's 'And oh – that the man I am might cease to be –' with Eliot's 'La Figlia che Piange', you will notice that relatively little part is played in Lawrence's poem by the sound of words. In 'La Figlia' it is all important. One becomes boring if one spells these things out too explicitly, but how subtle yet essential are the meanings conveyed by the succession of rhymes, 'pose', 'amaze', 'repose' in the last part of Eliot's poem, with their delicate dissonance and resolution of dissonance. (Even the contrast of 's' with 'z' seems to contribute.) What Eliot says of the 'auditory' imagination, the 'feeling for syllable and rhythm, penetrating far below the conscious levels of thought and feeling' is well illustrated here (see the Course Reader 'The Auditory Imagination'). They are not effects aimed at by Lawrence in his free verse. He said himself that what he was after 'doesn't depend on the ear, particularly, but on the sensitive soul'. And what this brings home to us is that such sound effects flourish most naturally in the presence of metre and rhyme. They depend on, or are helped by, some pattern of expectancy in the reader's mind or ear.

6.10 ■ Another point about the Lawrence poem. Does the epithet 'bluish' strike you as odd, in any way, in a poem?

Discussion

6.11 To me it reads like a *prose* epithet, deliberately flat and unevocative. It is more precise, in a way, than 'blue'; but from another point of view it is deliberately imprecise, implying 'for the purposes of this poem, it doesn't really matter all that much what precise shade the mountains were'. 'Bluish' is near enough. It does, on the contrary, matter how exactly darkness is to be envisaged, for darkness is the central subject of the poem, and accordingly Lawrence strikes out a very bold and imaginative metaphor: 'two valves of darkness'. But even this, to my mind, is a prose metaphor and would be quite at home in one of his novels. The feeling given to me by the poem is of a man straining every nerve to *explain* something; and explaining is something we associate more with prose than verse.■

WHAT PROSE AND VERSE ARE

6.12 ■ This brings us to the difference between prose and verse. Actually, I do not think it is at all a difficult question – unlike the difference between prose and poetry. Still, let us try to clear the matter up. How would you define the difference between prose and verse?

Discussion

6.13 I would define it as lying in the simple fact that verse, for some reason or other, is broken up into 'lines'. If you were to chop up some prose into 'lines', then you would have verse – I mean, you could read it as verse – though no doubt it would be dreadfully bad verse. The point about verse, I suggest, is that it is intrinsically – and not just historically – connected with singing. In singing, a singer has to take breath after every few notes, and the art of melody – that is to say, the art of balancing one completed musical phrase against another for emotional effect – grows out of this pausing for breath. Now, the 'lines' of verse are, in origin, merely an imitation of the strophes of sung melody. The fact that in verse, as opposed to conversation, you do not just go on, but make a regular or repeated pause – as you do, notionally, even at the end of a blank verse line – is a signal that what is going on is distantly related to singing. The poet is concerned with the physical or plastic qualities of the words he is using. He is expecting you to compare the shape of the line he has just spoken with that of the previous one, for the sake of some emotional effect, just as in musical melody. Thus, as I have said, if you chopped up a piece of prose into verse lines you would immediately read it, or try to read it, in a different way – which goes to show that we all of us know what 'verse' is. (A colleague says I am simplifying terribly here, and maybe he is right, so do not take this last paragraph as gospel. But I think it is one possible way of regarding the matter.)■

6.14 On the other hand we do not all know by instinct what 'poetry' is, as opposed to 'prose', and it may be a barren question. Mallarmé regarded as poetry any use of language which was not purely utilitarian, and that strikes me as not unreasonable. I bring him in here because, with Baudelaire, he was also the inventor of the 'prose-poem', that is to say a poem which is not written in verse. (Actually there were earlier precedents, but I will not trouble you with them here.) The prose-poem is a form which, from time to time, French poets have found very fruitful – for instance the most important work of Rimbaud was written in this form. Here is a translation of a prose-poem by Mallarmé.

Winter Shivering

This clock from Saxony which goes slow and strikes thirteen amid its flowers and its gods, to whom did it belong? Think that it came from Saxony by the long coaches in past times.

(Curious shadows hang on the worn windows.)

And your Venetian mirror, deep as a cold spring in a shore of tarnished serpents, who looked at themselves in it? Ah! I am sure that more than one woman has bathed her beauty's sin in this water; and perhaps, if I looked for long, I would see a naked ghost.

– You rogue, you often say wicked things.

(I see spiders' webs on top of the great casements.)

Our cupboard too is very old: see how this fire reddens its melancholy wood; the faded curtains are as old as it, and the embroidery of the chairs bare of paint, and the old engravings on the walls, and all our old things. Does it not even seem to you that the bengalees and the blue bird have faded with time?

(Do not think of the spiders' webs trembling on top of the great casements.)

You love all that, and that is why I can live beside you. Did you not wish, my sister, with the glance of times gone by, that in one of my poems these words should appear: 'the grace of faded things'? New objects displease you; you too they frighten with their shrill boldness, and you would feel the necessity of wearing them out, which is very difficult to do for those who do not enjoy action.

Come, shut your old German almanac, which you are reading with attention' although it appeared more than a hundred years ago and the kings it announces are all dead, and, lying on the ancient carpet with my head supported on your charitable knees in your faded dress, O calm child, I shall talk to you for hours; there are no more fields, and the streets are empty, I shall talk to you of our furniture . . . Your thoughts are wandering?

(Those spiders' webs shiver on top of the great casements.)

Of course, Mallarméan prose is almost as untranslatable as Mallarméan verse Still, I think this may give a sense of the character of the prose-poem, and how deliberately and even obtrusively it is using prose in a non-utilitarian way. This is sometimes a trouble for the ordinary reader, who tends to feel there is something 'precious' – airyfied, esoteric and cut off from ordinary experience – about the form, as if it were too keen to proclaim its own uselessness.

6.15 Or instead of 'ordinary reader' I should perhaps say 'English reader'; for the prose-poem has not on the whole flourished in English. Here is a prose-poem by T. S. Eliot – the only one in his *Collected Poems*.

Hysteria

As she laughed I was aware of becoming involved in her laughter and being part of it, until her teeth were only accidental stars with a talent for squad-drill. I was drawn in by short gasps, inhaled at each momentary recovery, lost finally in the dark caverns of her throat, bruised by the ripple of unseen muscles. An elderly waiter with trembling hands was hurriedly spreading a pink and white checked cloth over the rusty green iron table, saying: 'If the lady and gentleman wish to take their tea in the garden, if the lady and gentleman wish to take their tea in the garden . . .' I decided that if the shaking of her breasts could be stopped, some of the fragments of the afternoon might be collected, and I concentrated my attention with careful subtlety to this end.

■ What is your reaction to this? Do you consider 'poem' a good term to describe it?

Discussion

6.16 I am not, myself, much more eager to define a 'poem' than I am to define 'modernism'. Nevertheless I have a feeling that 'poem' or 'prose-poem' is not an ideal name for this; at any rate it is very unlike Mallarmé's prose-poems. It reads almost like an extract from an unwritten novel. And I would very much like to read the novel. It is a compelling piece of writing, however we classify it.■

THE PROSE OF FICTION

6.17 This brings me to an important point. We should never forget, when considering the development of twentieth-century verse, that extraordinary, and in many ways very similar, developments took place in the same period in prose fiction. Thus, when I said that Lawrence's diction seemed to me a 'prose' diction, I meant no derogation at all to prose: for the diction of Lawrence's novels is a most remarkable invention, with little in common with the prose of a *Times* or *Guardian* leader. So, perhaps even more, is the prose of James Joyce – it is much more 'advanced' than his verse. 'Modernist' prose fiction has no reason at all to feel inferior to 'modernist' verse, indeed it influenced 'modernist' verse; yet on the other hand it *is* prose, it is not prose trying to be poetry, or that rather bogus thing 'poetic' prose. The point is clearly illustrated by Joyce. Particularly so, because in 1914 or thereabouts he wrote a strange work known as *Giacomo Joyce*. I have a particular affection for *Giacomo Joyce*, which, for various reasons, had to wait for publication till 1968 and, to my mind, has not yet had quite the recognition it deserves. It seems to me a masterpiece, and a masterpiece exactly to the prescriptions of Ezra Pound – though he never read it – and it provides a striking parallel to the Imagist verse of the period. It is a novel, a novel about a love affair, mostly make-believe, between Joyce and a Jewish pupil of his in Trieste. But it is a novel which in the printed text only occupies sixteen pages, much of which remain blank; and though it is in prose, the prose is as concentrated and difficult as any 'modernist' verse. Joyce comes close to the methods of the Imagists in it. He ruthlessly cuts away all connecting matter, so that what

remains seems as dense and solid almost as a physical object. So much is this so, that he can convey meaning by the way the paragraphs are laid out on the page and the amount of blank space between them.

6.18 Here are its opening paragraphs.

Who? A pale face surrounded by heavy odorous furs. Her movements are shy and nervous. She uses quizzing-glasses.
Yes: a brief syllable. A brief laugh. A brief beat of the eyelids.

Cobweb handwriting, traced long and fine with quiet disdain and resignation: a young person of quality.

I launch forth on an easy wave of tepid speech: Swedenborg, the pseudo-Areopagite, Miguel de Molinos, Joachim Abbas. The wave is spent. Her classmate, retwisting her twisted body, purrs in boneless Viennese Italian: *Che coltura!* The long eyelids beat and lift: a burning needleprick stings and quivers in the velvet iris.

High heels clack hollow on the resonant stone stairs. Wintry air in the castle, gibbeted coats of mail, rude iron sconces over the windings of the winding turret stairs. Tapping clacking heels, a high and hollow noise. There is one below would speak with your ladyship.

She never blows her nose. A form of speech: the lesser for the greater.

Rounded and ripened: rounded by the lathe of inter-marriage and ripened in the forcing-house of the seclusion of her race.

A ricefield near Vercelli under creamy summer haze. The wings of her drooping hat shadow her false smile. Shadows streak her falsely smiling face, smitten by the hot creamy light, grey wheyhued shadows under the jawbones, streaks of eggyolk yellow on the moistened brow, rancid yellow humour lurking within the softened pulp of the eyes.

A flower given by her to my daughter. Frail gift, frail giver, frail blue-veined child.

40

Padua far beyond the sea. The silent middle age, night, darkness of history sleep in the *Piazza delle Erbe* under the moon. The city sleeps. Under the arches in the dark streets near the river the whores' eyes spy out for fornicators. *Cinque servizi per cinque franchi*. A dark wave of sense, again and again and again.

> *Mine eyes fail in darkness, mine eyes fail,*
> *Mine eyes fail in darkness, love.*

Again. No more. Dark love, dark longing. No more. Darkness.

6.19 I want to call *Giacomo Joyce* a novel, because it has the range of a novel. But at all events it is not a prose-poem. For the prose of fiction can hardly be called 'non-utilitarian': it has one obvious use or function, which is to tell a story. Joyce's prose, in its elliptical but efficacious way, tells a story even in *Giacomo Joyce*. I have brought this work in (though I could have made the point almost equally well from Joyce's *Ulysses* or fiction by other 'modernist' writers) to emphasize that, if we are mapping the territories of traditional verse, free verse and the prose-poem, we need also to trace the frontiers they all possess with prose fiction.

7 OBSCURITY IN 'MODERNIST' VERSE

7.1 It would be foolish to pretend that 'modernist' poetry is not sometimes very difficult and obscure. Readers at the time felt this more strongly than we do now, for they were suspicious that they might be being hoaxed. Anyway, such problems tend to be resolved by time and familiarity. But on the other hand, familiarity may breed contempt, which is a bad thing. 'Modernist' poems not only were, but are, obscure, and their obscurity is often fruitful and a clue to what is valuable in them. It would be wrong to wave it away, as matter that no longer concerns us; though it is a mistake, too, to be frightened by it.

7.2 In the Course Reader we have reprinted Eliot's helpful note on 'Difficult Poetry', written in 1933. However, it might be worth my adding a few remarks. What I would like to do is to define a few categories of obscurity. This may make the problem more manageable.

SYMBOLISTE OBSCURITY

7.3 The point about this type of obscurity, as I have suggested earlier, is that it is intrinsic to the whole enterprise of *Symboliste* writing, it being one of its tenets that meaning in a poem can never be expressed directly. In this course we shall most often encounter *Symboliste* obscurity, on the part of English poets at least, in T. S. Eliot; and a point to remember is that lines that seem at first sight hopelessly obscure in Eliot may seem much less so in the context of the whole poem. For this reason: in each poem, Eliot tends to establish one particular style of obscurity, which becomes the convention or formula for that poem. The obscurity of 'Prufrock' is very different from that of 'The Hollow Men'. There is also a contrary point: his poems often appear at first sight *more* straightforward and rational than they are. A few years ago there was a lengthy controversy in the periodical *Essays in Criticism* about the interpretation of Eliot's 'A Cooking Egg' – and very weird some of the interpretations were. But my point is, it is a poem about which one tends to feel that, with just a bit more luck or a bit more patience, we will have it licked and be left with a straightforward statement or anecdote on our hands. This is a delusion I am sure.

OBSCURITY OF ALLUSION

7.4 Extending what I said about Yeats's 'Who Goes with Fergus' (paras. 3.24, 3.26): if you feel that you need a dozen reference books to hand before you can begin to appreciate a particular poem, the odds are that you are reading the poem wrongly. What is true, though, in the case of Yeats, is that it may be a help to read round in other poems of his, since you are likely to find the same, or similar, symbols or trains of thought turning up again and again in slightly different guise. Yeats may even be depending on our doing so, and if so, it is not an unreasonable demand. The problem of allusion becomes acute with Ezra Pound, but we shall have to postpone discussion of that until Unit 6.

WITTY OBSCURITY

7.5 This is obscurity which is meant to be solved, like a puzzle. The enjoyment of the poem, to a large extent, lies in 'solving' it and appreciating the poet's cleverness. Of course, not *only* in that, for cleverness must have some purpose: but this is the first step. Consider these two lines from William Empson's 'Bacchus', in his volume *The Gathering Storm* (1940):

> The god arkitect whose coping with the Flood
> Groyned the white stallion arches of the main.

■ Empson is cramming as many verbal ambiguities into these lines as he possibly can, partly just for the fun of it, and it is up to us to disentangle them. You might like to try it as an exercise.

Discussion

7.6 I can spot the following: 'arkitect' ('architect'; and 'roofer of the Ark' – 'tectum' is the Latin for 'roof'); 'coping' ('managing'; and 'coping' in the architectural sense of an overhanging ledge of masonry); 'Groyned' (a 'groyn or breakwater'; and 'groin'); 'white stallion arches' (the stallions' groin, which is arch-shaped; but also an allusion to 'white horses', i.e. the foam on the top of waves).■

'SHOCK TACTICS' OBSCURITY

7.7 What do you make of the following poem by Dylan Thomas, a poet of the second generation of 'modernists' (it was first published in 1939)?

Because the pleasure-bird whistles after the hot wires,
Shall the blind horse sing sweeter?
Convenient bird and beast lie lodged to suffer
The supper and knives of a mood.
In the sniffed and poured snow on the tip of the tongue of the year
That clouts the spittle like bubbles with broken rooms,
An enamoured man alone by the twigs of his eyes, two fires,
Camped in the drug-white shower of nerves and food,
Savours the lick of the times through a deadly wood of hair
In a wind that plucked a goose,
Nor ever, as the wild tongue breaks its tombs,
Rounds to look at the red, wagged root.
Because there stands, one story out of the bum city,
That frozen wife whose juices drift like a fixed sea
Secretly in statuary,
Shall I, struck on the hot and rocking street,
Not spin to stare at an old year
Toppling and burning in the muddle of towers and galleries
Like the mauled pictures of boys?
The salt person and blasted place
I furnish with the meat of a fable;
If the dead starve, their stomachs turn to tumble
An upright man in the antipodes
Or spray-based and rock-chested sea:
Over the past table I repeat this present grace.

Not much, perhaps, at a first or second reading. However, my comment, which is by no means entirely a hostile one, would be that we can be sure that Thomas does not expect us to make much plain sense of it. He depends on our bafflement. To be sure, as we read and re-read the poem, we may with luck get the hang of what it is saying – for Dylan Thomas is usually, though I think not always, 'saying' something. Still, we realize pretty soon that his verse is obscure not so much because what he is saying is obscure and difficult – for it is often something rather simple – but because he likes it that way: he wants to astonish, to electrify and bamboozle. When we read those startling and powerful opening lines

Because the pleasure-bird whistles after the hot wires
Shall the blind horse sing sweeter . . .

we do not feel we are expected to understand them fully. And when we learn that there is, or was, a practice of blinding song-birds with hot wires, we do not feel 'Well, I should have guessed that'; we feel 'I couldn't possibly have been *expected* to know that.'

7.8 I was tempted to sub-title this category 'Surrealist obscurity', had Dylan Thomas not denied that he was a Surrealist. However if you happen to know any of the painters of the Surrealist school, like Max Ernst or Magritte, you will see a resemblance. They do not merely employ shock tactics, as many artists do, they depend on them. Shock tactics, the bouncing of the spectator out of his accustomed logical habits, are essential to their technique. In Unit 13 you will be studying the French poet Guillaume Apollinaire who sometimes practised shock tactics of this kind, and who, as a matter of fact, was the inventor of the term 'Surrealism'.

ILLEGITIMATE OBSCURITY

7.9   I have put this category in to remind you that one does not have humbly to swallow every sort of obscurity. There is a kind which is the result of sheer incompetence. It is really just another name for bad verse – but bad verse of a particularly twentieth-century sort; for in most previous ages a poet, however bad he was, had at least to make sense. I do not feel like giving an example of bad verse of this kind – though it would be easy – for two reasons. First, whereas the reasons why a poem is good are always instructive and worth seeking, the reasons why a poem is worthless are not very interesting; if you say 'incompetence' you have said almost enough. Secondly, I might be wrong about the poem; and at least, the poet ought to be allowed a fair trial, which would mean taking other poems of his into account, as they might throw new light on his meaning.

Figure 6   Bicycle wheel (1913–64) by Marcel Duchamp, discussed by
Norbert Lynton in the television programme 'Making It New'
(Schwarz galleria d'arte, Milan © A.D.A.G.P. 1975)

8 WAS 'MODERNISM' A GOOD THING?

8.1 This is a question which is sometimes asked, so I suppose one ought to have an answer ready, and my own would emphatically be 'Yes, very much a good thing.' I find the best 'modernist' art, the art of Eliot and Joyce and Picasso and Stravinsky, intensely exciting and even have difficulty in understanding those who do not share my feeling. However, plague and earthquake and atomic warfare are exciting, so that cannot be quite enough recommendation. Let me therefore list one or two arguments used by those who do *not* think 'modernism' was a good thing. They say, for instance:

a That the advent of 'modernist' influences from America and Europe, and the extraordinary dominance over English literary culture exercised for twenty years by Eliot, in his double role of poet and critic, interrupted a native tradition, associated especially with Thomas Hardy, that in the long run was of more value.

b That 'modernist' poetry and art is impossibly highbrow, élitist and remote from the business of ordinary living. That it encourages culture snobbery and caused a damaging division between highbrow and popular culture.

c That 'modernist' art uses impossibly bad manners towards the reader or spectator – that indeed it makes no effort at all to 'communicate'.

d That 'modernist' art seems to go with reactionary and authoritarian politics, which is in itself a damning judgement upon it.

e That it seems to ask the reader to trespass into dangerous areas of his own unconscious. It incites him to prize extremism of every kind at the expense of the civilized virtues of order, decency and moderation.

8.2 These are serious and not absurd charges. However I do not feel this is the moment either for me to try to answer them or for you to make up your mind about them. It would be a good moment, though, to have a look at the essays grouped under the heading 'Modernism' in the Course Reader, where you will find some of these accusations argued at length.

9 'MODERNISM' AND THE WAR

9.1 So often has one read of that cloudless summer of 1914, and of how far from anyone's thoughts was a European war. And how false it is! It is one of those many myths that cluster round the 1914–18 war, and as with most myths its meaning is worth exploring.

9.2 The truth is, for twenty years, the British, the French and the Germans had all been obsessed by the prospect of war. They feared it, they desired it, they planned for it, joked about it and wrote about it. There was a fashion for 'invasion literature' in Edwardian Britain. Popular novels were published in which the heroes progressed from schooldays to war – a war which they would fight in the spirit of the school playing field. Wells, whose favourite private pastime was the 'war game', wove science fiction round cataclysmic world conflicts.

9.3 What I think was happening, too, was that already, before the war had occurred, people were saddling it with responsibility for disagreeable social changes. A certain class in British society, those living off modest inherited incomes, guessed subconsciously that their status was declining, and they constructed a scenario according to which they sacrificed all for their country's sake. The 'gentleman' would die in foreign fields, and the 'Jew' and the 'profiteer' would inherit.

9.4 Altogether, golden age though it may have seemed in retrospect, the Edwardian age was a very self-divided and uneasy one. It was preparing for war without knowing it was doing so. Its official culture was curiously out of gear with reality: it was patriotic – like, shall we say, Kipling – with a bluster that concealed disquiet; or it was socially-minded – like, shall we say, Galsworthy – in a way that displayed disquiet merely for the sake of doing so. (Samuel Hynes has put this well in *The Edwardian Turn of Mind*: 'When he, Galsworthy, brought injustice into a story, he did so in a way that was neither objective nor didactic but simply emotional; and his motive in doing so was not the alleviation of injustice but the alleviation of emotion.') There was, it is true, an admirable body of philanthropic Liberal thinkers, addressing the problems of social injustice with high-minded zeal. But somehow, as we feel now, they were too blinkered by class assumptions to see the problems clearly. A little more good will, a few more blue books, reports and sociological surveys and, so they felt, all would be well: Old England, juster and more efficient but substantially unaltered, would continue its allotted role in history. Meanwhile, in the years just before the war, the country was almost paralysed by strikes and women's suffrage agitation and seemed to be nearing a civil war over Ireland; and every year just before 1914 the country lost more by emigration than it was to lose by death during each year of the war itself.

9.5 The point I am leading up to is that 'modernist' writers, in attacking established English culture for sloppiness of mind, sentimentality and self-deception, seem in retrospect to have had much justification. For instance, that weekend pastoralism which they condemned in the Georgian poets was – they were right – a self-deceiving affair, and an apt counterpart to the equally self-deceiving 'back-to-the-land' policies of political Liberalism. Again, that hymning by poets like Newbolt of healthiness and patriotism and schoolboy ethics was self-deceiving; it was the disguise for various fears, including the fear of Germany. And, once again, that assumption by Georgian poets (see para. 5.2) that they belonged to a 'timeless' tradition of English poetry was another self-deception. The 'modernist' poets, in demanding more intelligence, more honesty, more austerity and self-discipline and true energy – the energy of the craftsman – were calling for qualities which were badly needed in the present state of Britain. One can argue that they were more farseeing and had a firmer sense of realities than professional politicians and social critics. If one thinks of fiction rather than verse for a moment, how much more successful were *avant-garde* writers like Joyce and Lawrence than middlebrow writers like Wells and Bennett in depicting working-class and lower-middle-class life without facetiousness or romanticization or embarrassment. Likewise it was 'modernist' artists and writers who managed to bring to consciousness the growing desire for violence in the pre-war European mind. Yeats expresses, obscurely, something of this recognition in his poem 'The Magi', published in 1914:

> Now as at all times I can see in the mind's eye,
> In their stiff, painted clothes, the pale unsatisfied ones
> Appear and disappear in the blue depths of the sky
> With all their ancient faces like rain-beaten stones,
> And all their helms of silver hovering side by side,
> And all their eyes still fixed, hoping to find once more,
> Being by Calvary's turbulence unsatisfied,
> The uncontrollable mystery on the bestial floor.

The message was more openly proclaimed in Stravinsky's *The Rite of Spring*, with its celebration of orgiastic human sacrifice – a work which caused an uproar on its first performance in Paris in 1913. It may be held that in meddling with such dark forces, art was performing a dangerous function. This is an issue we shall have to return to; but at least, I think we can agree, what these artists were doing was more responsible than the sabre-rattling of the *Daily Mail*.

9.6   Thus, if we are looking for the relationship between the war and 'modernism', I think we should look to this pre-war period. The most significant feature of the relationship was the way 'modernist' art interpreted the deeper needs and weaknesses of the pre-war age. I would add, though, that, to my mind, the finest poem about the war, the most complete human and intellectual response to it, was by a 'modernist'. I am thinking of those two brief sections in Ezra Pound's *Hugh Selwyn Mauberley* (1920):

IV

These fought in any case,
and some believing,
                    pro domo, in any case . . .

Some quick to arm,
some for adventure,
some from fear of weakness,
some from fear of censure,
some for love of slaughter, in imagination,
learning later . . .
some in fear, learning love of slaughter;

Died some, pro patria,
                    non 'dulce' non 'et decor' . . .
walked eye-deep in hell
believing in old men's lies, then unbelieving
came home, home to a lie,
home to many deceits,
home to old lies and new infamy;
usury age-old and age-thick
and liars in public places.

Daring as never before, wastage as never before.
Young blood and high blood,
fair cheeks, and fine bodies;

fortitude as never before

frankness as never before,
disillusions as never told in the old days,
hysterias, trench confessions,
laughter out of dead bellies.

V

There died a myriad,
And of the best, among them,
For an old bitch gone in the teeth,
For a botched civilization,

Charm, smiling at the good mouth,
Quick eyes gone under earth's lid,

For two gross of broken statues,
For a few thousand battered books.

47

All Pound's mania for good art and rancorous impatience with public stupidity had not – yet, at least – destroyed his human sympathies. In this poem he weighs art against human life and finds it lighter in the scale. One feels that he had genuinely weighed the two; and his measured and indignant irony in that 'few thousand battered books' – which no doubt is meant to include his own books – is wonderfully balanced and fine. (The sense, I think, is 'Even if the war *were* being fought on behalf of culture, which of course it isn't, what does culture amount to when weighed against the human waste?') It is so different from the hysteria with which Kipling would glee-fully have hurled art and culture overboard. Of course, Pound was an American and a non-combatant, so perhaps judiciousness came easier to him. And it is true, too, that in the years after the war, hysteria against 'usury age-old and age-thick/and liars in public places' overtook him and he lost his balance catastrophically. Nevertheless, this poem says much for the strength of 'modernist' attitudes.

9.7 There is, to my mind, less to be said about the *effect* of the war on 'modernist' poetry. As 'modernists', these writers were confirmed in their beliefs and diagnoses by the war and strengthened in their determination to 'Make it New'. As men, the war affected them deeply, as it did everyone, but in diverse ways, which it is not very helpful to generalize about. From the point of view of the history of poetry, perhaps the clearest fruit of the war was the attitude of the young Auden to English society. Auden assaulted English cosiness with a blithe, bloody-minded, intellectually arro-gant impatience which is the pre-war 'modernist' attitude shorn of its aestheticism and toughened by memory of the war.

9.8 Where the war had major impact on English poetry was in another sphere – that is to say, in its effect on certain 'Georgian' poets, especially Wilfred Owen. It was this overwhelming event which, in a quite direct sense, 'made' Wilfred Owen as a poet. And at this point I hand over the argument to Arnold Kettle.

THE WAR POETS

1.1 I would like, in this section, to take up Nick Furbank's last sentences and examine them in more detail. My chief aims will be (a) to discuss the ways in which Wilfred Owen's attitude to poetry change as a result of the First World War and (b) to offer some thoughts on the relation between 'modernist' developments and those others, like Owen's, which do not lie happily within the usual scope of the term 'modernist'. I should stress that I am not attempting to give an overall account of the poetry of the First World War. For further discussion of this poetry see the passage from Jon Silkin's *Out of Battle: the Poetry of the Great War* in the Course Reader.

1.2 It is common knowledge that a generation of poets who fought in the war of 1914–18 were led to write poetry in some ways strikingly different from the poetry most widely read in the earlier years of the century, whether we refer to 'neo-Romantic', 'Edwardian' or 'Georgian' poetry. Siegfried Sassoon and Isaac Rosenberg are the names which, apart from Owen's, spring most readily to mind. I propose to concentrate on Owen because Sassoon's poetry (though I do not want to undervalue it) seems by comparison a little thin and Rosenberg's *changed* much less than Owen's as a result of his war experience and he is therefore of less significance as a case study. Owen was not only the most talented but the most influential of the war poets. You find, by 1934, C. Day Lewis referring to him in *A Hope for Poetry* (see Course Reader) as one of the three principal 'ancestors' of the poets of the 'thirties (Hopkins and Eliot were the others). 'Owen was not a technical revolutionary', Day Lewis wrote, 'his one innovation is the constant use of alliterative assonance as an end rhyme – (mystery, mastery; killed, cold). But he was a true revolutionary poet, opening up new fields of sensitiveness for his successors.'

1.3 I am not implying – in concentrating for a moment on the 'war poets' – that the effects of the war on poetry were confined to these poets (I agree with Nick Furbank that Yeats, Pound and Eliot – to say nothing of Hardy and Lawrence – responded to the war deeply and significantly); nor do I think it possible to treat the 1914–18 war in isolation from the other social and cultural developments of the early twentieth century. But it is worth emphasizing that the first distinctive feature of the relationship of Owen, Sassoon and Rosenberg to the war was that they actually fought in it, actually spent those appalling years in and out of the trenches (Owen was killed on 4 November 1918) and consciously modified their attitudes to poetry as a result. When Owen uses the word 'France' in his poetry it means only one thing and has nothing to do with troubadours or courtly love or Rimbaud or Baudelaire or the cultural associations upon which other poets play.

1.4 I propose first to ask you to read two poems in juxtaposition. First, one written a few months after the beginning of the war, the other a few months before the end. The problems involved in making such a comparison can be complex and I do not want to avoid all the complexities: but my primary purpose is not to make a critical comparison of either the individual poems or the kinds of poetry they represent. My main point, on which I would like you to focus, is simply to make a straightforward, even obvious, contrast between the attitudes to poetry implicit in the two poems. So, though I shall subsequently discuss some of the literary-critical implications (and dangers) about making such a comparison, I hope you will concentrate first on the wood rather than the trees and look at the two poems in a straightforward, not too sophisticated way.

1.5 The first is by Rupert Brooke and it was written in 1914.

The Dead

Blow out, you bugles, over the rich Dead!
   There's none of these so lonely and poor of old,
    But, dying, has made us rarer gifts than gold.
These laid the world away; poured out the red
Sweet wine of youth; gave up the years to be
   Of work and joy, and that unhoped serene,
    That men call age; and those who would have been,
Their sons, they gave, their immortality.

Blow, bugles, blow! They brought us, for our dearth,
   Holiness, lacked so long, and Love, and Pain.
Honour has come back, as a king, to earth,
   And paid his subjects with a royal wage;
And Nobleness walks in our ways again;
   And we have come into our heritage.

1.6   The second, by Wilfred Owen, was written three years later.

Dulce et Decorum Est

Bent double, like old beggars under sacks,
Knock-kneed, coughing like hags, we cursed through sludge,
Till on the haunting flares we turned our backs,
And towards our distant rest began to trudge.
Men marched asleep. Many had lost their boots,
But limped on, blood-shod. All went lame, all blind;
Drunk with fatigue; deaf even to the hoots
Of gas-shells dropping softly behind.

Gas! GAS! Quick, boys! – An ecstasy of fumbling,
Fitting the clumsy helmets just in time,
But someone still was yelling out and stumbling
And floundering like a man in fire or lime. –
Dim through the misty panes and thick green light,
As under a green sea, I saw him drowning.

In all my dreams before my helpless sight
He plunges at me, guttering, choking, drowning.

If in some smothering dreams, you too could pace
Behind the wagon that we flung him in,
And watch the white eyes writhing in his face,
His hanging face, like a devil's sick of sin;
If you could hear, at every jolt, the blood
Come gargling from the froth-corrupted lungs,
Bitter as the cud
Of vile, incurable sores on innocent tongues, –
My friend, you would not tell with such high zest
To children ardent for some desperate glory,
The old Lie: Dulce et decorum est
Pro patria mori.

■ The statement I would like you to think about and jot down your response to – i.e. whether you agree or disagree and why – is 'The Rupert Brooke poem could scarcely have been written much after 1914: the Wilfred Owen poem could not possibly have been written before 1914.'

Discussion

1.7 I suspect that most people will (even if with some reservations) agree with the statement. 'The Dead' may not be one of Brooke's best poems but it is surely a fair example of the sort of thing that could be expected from a war poem of about 1914. You may like it or not, but if you had read it when it first came out you certainly would not have been *surprised* by it. The sentiments it expresses and the language in which they are expressed belong to a tradition of which it is a fair – if not a very distinguished – example. And one has only to ask oneself the question: 'Could it have been written in, say, 1939 or 1940, near the beginning of the Second World War?' to recognize that the style had by that time gone hopelessly out-of-date. I do not mean that it is absolutely inconceivable that a poem of this type could be written after 1914, for there is always a hangover of totally unoriginal and derivative verse of the sort no one can take seriously (like most of the verses on Christmas cards, etc.). But a poet of the calibre of Rupert Brooke would not have written it.

1.8 The question 'why' is more complex and I propose to leave it for the moment. You may have felt that what 'dated' Brooke's poem was the nature of the feelings expressed or you may have thought it was the language or style or even the 'genre' (the *kind* of poem). Let's come back to that in a moment and consider meanwhile the second part of the statement.

1.9 Some people will no doubt have agreed with the part of the statement which deals with the Owen poem on the grounds of purely historical evidence. Gas attacks and the kind of warfare described in the poem belong historically to the First World War. True enough. But even if the poem had contained less specific evidence of that sort there would still be little doubt that it belonged to the post-1914 era. Not because it is a war poem: there had been plenty of those in the nineteenth century (one has only to think of 'The Battle of Blenheim' or 'The Charge of the Light Brigade'). Not even because the language is colloquial and 'realistic': so is Kipling's. Not because it queries patriotism of the accepted kind: earlier poets had done that (in any case one should take care here: Owen is not in this poem making a direct political attack on the waging of the war). No, what takes this poem indubitably into the post-1914 world is its *style*: the way language is used (not *utterly* different from its use by earlier poets, yet new), the particular sort of bitterness which involves a shifting of the poet's sense of commitment, the combination of personal experience with a 'public' theme, above all the sense that nothing need be excluded from poetry and that poetry exacts no special attitude to what is 'poetic'.

1.10 Let us pursue our comparison between the two poems a bit further.

1.11 It is always difficult to compare two poems because they are seldom doing precisely the same thing. In particular two separate problems tend to get mixed up: the artistic quality of each of the poems and the question of the *sort* of poems they are. Yet to avoid all such comparisons is also difficult, for it can lead one to evade the important, though very complex, questions of the possible relationships between quality and kind or between value and context. I do not propose to try to tackle these, except perhaps obliquely.

1.12 ■ Looking back at 'The Dead', how would you describe the *kind* or category of poem it belongs to and some of the main attitudes to poetry it presupposes?

Discussion

1.13 It is a public poem (and, in one sense, relatively 'impersonal'), of the sort written (by a poet laureate for instance) for an occasion. It is also very 'general' in its approach to its subject matter. Although there may no doubt be a strong personal emotion behind it, it is a shared, public emotion and the poem does not attempt to express any very new, intense, personal insights of a surprising kind. On the contrary the imagery is 'conventional' (I am not using the word in a pejorative sense, but simply to indicate that it operates within an accepted tradition or convention). For instance the bugle call at the beginning at once recalls an accepted form of ceremonial. Anyone old enough to remember Armistice Day between the wars will know the associations and how they worked. This is a poem which could appropriately have been recited at the unveiling of a war memorial.

1.14 Poetry of this kind depends for its effect on a shared tradition, an acceptance in this case of certain attitudes, with a long history behind them, to 'the nation'. And the style or rhetoric the poet uses is bound up with this. Phrases like 'rarer gifts than gold', 'these laid the world away', 'the red sweet wine of youth' are of the sort the reader or listener *expects* to hear and he does not feel impelled to ask whether they are 'realistic' in the sense of being accurate descriptions of what getting killed in a war is actually like. I use the word 'rhetoric' neutrally to indicate a way of using language felt to be appropriate to the situation concerned. But, for the very reason that rhetoric *is* 'a way of using language felt to be appropriate to the situation concerned', the word is seldom used quite neutrally, and perhaps cannot be, for 'what is felt to be appropriate' is always changing, and one man's or class's or tradition's sense of appropriateness can be another's poison. When people object to a certain use of language as 'rhetorical' what they usually mean is that they are unsympathetic to the purposes for which it is being used. The word 'rhetoric' itself becomes a battleground. This is an important point to grasp in relation to 'modernist' trends in poetry. Rimbaud, Pound, Yeats, Auden all habitually use the word 'rhetoric' in a pejorative sense to indicate a style they feel has become intolerable. Auden says of Rimbaud that 'in that child the rhetorician's lie/Burst like a pipe.' The word 'rhetoric' is like the word 'propaganda'. If you resent an author's aims you call his writing propagandist; if you go along with his aims or are won over to them by his writing, you feel you have had a rewarding experience. Rhetoric that succeeds is seldom described as rhetoric.

1.15 The contrast between 'The Dead' and 'Dulce et Decorum Est' is in one sense a contrast of styles or rhetoric. But it is not a 'purely literary' contrast. Behind the contrasting styles lie contrasting attitudes to the world, contrasting personal experiences, and contrasting assumptions about the role of poetry. That is why, in one sense comparisons between the two poems are bound to be unsatisfactory; and also why we cannot make any useful comparison without a special emphasis on the *context* of the poems. I do not believe it is possible to separate one's response to these poems from one's knowledge that one was written in the first flush of enthusiasm in 1914 by a young man who had not yet seen much of what the war was actually like, while the other was written by a young man who had been through gas attacks and the whole atrocious experience of three years of trench warfare. The two poems arise out of different historical situations. It is impossible to believe that, had Rupert Brooke lived (he died on 23 February 1915), he would, by 1917, have written a poem in which bleeding to death in war would be referred to as pouring out 'the red sweet wine of youth'.

1.16 What I refer to as a contrast in 'context' is not adequately described in terms of different kinds of poetry or different ideas about the war. It is true that Brooke implies that he is 'for' the war, which is seen as bringing back honour and holiness into the British way of life; but Owen does not say he is against the war. He is not saying that it is wrong to die for your country (or right, for that matter). What he is concerned to convey is that people should not fool themselves or others about what dying in the war actually means. Like many of Owen's poems it is directed not so much against the war as a political act or policy as against the complacency and hypocrisy of those 'at home' who present it as something other than it is.

1.17 Nor is the tendency of a reader today to compare Brooke's poem unfavourably with Owen's to be explained simply in terms of changing fashions about the *sort* of poetry that is admired and a rejection of public, 'occasional', celebratory poems of this kind. It is true of course that in a less secure society, in which there are strong class and ideological divisions and in which appeals for 'national unity' consequently have a hollow ring, it is much harder for a poet to speak with a 'public voice' that will find general acceptance than it was in 1914 (though it is also true that one of the main ways that we have become aware of disintegration and insecurity is by our discovery through our use of language of what is hollow and what rings true).

1.18 It is true that public poems of celebration or exhortation have gone out of fashion in twentieth-century Britain. The role of poet laureate has itself become problematic. For these changes there are cogent historical reasons; but I do not propose to go into them. I am chiefly concerned to combat the argument that 'The Dead' is nowadays a less acceptable poem than 'Dulce et Decorum Est' simply because it is of a kind or genre we no longer like; for I think that is a simplification which can be misleading. What is wrong with 'The Dead' is not the 'kind' it belongs to, but something more specific. There is nothing wrong with public poems of a polemical kind as such. Take for example another, older sonnet: Milton's poem 'On the late Massacre in Piemont' written in 1655.

> Avenge O Lord thy slaughter'd Saints, whose bones
>   Lie scatter'd on the Alpine mountains cold,
>   Ev'n them who kept thy truth so pure of old
>   When all our Fathers worship't Stocks and Stones,
> Forget not: in thy book record their groanes
>   Who were thy Sheep and in their antient Fold
>   Slayn by the bloody *Piemontese* that roll'd
>   Mother with Infant down the Rocks. Their moans
> The Vales redoubl'd to the Hills, and they
>   To Heav'n. Their martyr'd blood and ashes sow
>   O're all th'*Italian* fields where still doth sway
> The triple Tyrant: that from these may grow
>   A hunder'd-fold, who having learnt thy way
>   Early may fly the *Babylonian* wo.

Now this is a public, polemical poem of an extreme and uncompromising kind and its style involves a rhetoric not readily sympathetic to latter-day readers. Yet I doubt whether many such readers would want to dispute the power or splendour of Milton's poem or its ability to communicate its intensities of feeling to readers who care little enough – in the abstract – about the issues of seventeenth-century Piedmontese history or who do not specially warm to calls for vengeance. And, speaking for myself, I think the reason I find Milton's sonnet much more moving than Brooke's is that Milton succeeds in embodying in the language of his poem a full sense of the energy – physical and moral – which the events he is evoking involved. The Piedmont sonnet, in other words, manages to combine the striking energy and realism characteristic of Owen's poem with the 'occasional' public polemic relevant to Brooke's and we feel no lurking doubts about either the 'genre', the nature of the 'message' or the quality of the rhetoric. (My purpose in making this short diversion is not to compare Brooke unfavourably with Milton qua poet, but to block the too easy response to 'The Dead' that 'we don't like that sort of poetry any more'.)

1.19 The trouble with 'The Dead', as it seems to me, is not that either its subject matter or its style as such is illegitimate, but that – because of some inner failure in conviction of the poet's – neither is brought into play in a manner which can win over the

Figure 7 Wilfred Owen and small boy (Courtesy Imperial War
Museum and Oxford University Press).

reader. And the conclusion seems inescapable that Brooke was writing a poem which
on some deep level he did not sufficiently believe in. It is the inadequacy of the rhetoric
that is the give-away.

1.20 What is intolerable to most of us, I suppose, is the gap between the poetic sensibility
Brooke's poem displays and the truth about the war we have come, partly as a result
of our experience of poetry like Owen's, to recognize. It is not just the bland imagery
of the first part of the sonnet that is inadequate: it is the use of those abstract nouns,
dignified by a capital letter, in the sestet. Now there is no earthly reason (despite Ezra
Pound's exhortations) why poets should not use abstract nouns. Shakespeare uses them
all the time. But there is – as the 'modernists' recognized – a danger in it: that, though
they may appear to be timeless and universal, in fact they are liable to date rather
quickly. One generation's or one class's idea of love or honour is not necessarily
another's. So the poet who goes in for a great many abstract nouns does well to make
sure that they are, so to speak, fully supported by specific and more concrete words
(so that their precise meaning and significance are made clear) or else by ensuring
that they are used speculatively, with due allowance for the ambiguities which time
and social change rather quickly deck them with. I think it has to be said that
Brooke's use of abstractions in this poem is highly vulnerable. It is not clear in what
sense 'Honour has come back, as a king, to earth'; but it *is* clear from the tone that
the reader is not being asked to speculate about the assertion. We are not asked to
recall what, for instance, Falstaff had to say on the subject.

1.21 In other words, the poet is playing too easily on stock responses associated with
social attitudes which have not stood up to the test of longer-term experience. For
the word 'noble' to bear analysis in such a context it must surely at least include a
coming to terms with the 'froth-corrupted lungs' of Owen's poem. As it is, that
whole final section of the second poem acts as a kind of gas attack on the poetic
trenches in which the earlier poet has dug himself. The 'my friend' whom Owen
speaks to might be the ghost of Rupert Brooke. And we remember, perhaps, the
striking line from Owen's 'Strange Meeting':

I am the enemy you killed, my friend.

In that single line there is embodied a complexity of experience, and a humanity, which Brooke, with his all too naive high-mindedness, could not allow into his poem: and this is a matter not simply of the overall conception of the poem (what, in a general way, it is 'about') but of the way he uses words. Compare Brooke's use of the words 'king' and 'subjects' in 'The Dead' with Owen's use of words like 'beggars' and 'friend' and 'children'; or Brooke's image of pouring out the wine with Owen's word 'blood-shod'. With Owen the more these words sink into your mind the more they mean: with Brooke it is not unfair to say that the metaphor actually detracts from the force of what he is saying because it has no inner appropriateness.

1.22   It is tempting to say of Brooke's poem that it simply is not very good as poetry; but I do not think one can quite leave it at that. What happens with 'The Dead', it seems to me, is that a number of attitudes about what poetry is, the sort of thing to be expected of a poem and the sort of language a poet is expected to write in, are (more or less unconsciously) invoked and fail to do what is required of them. What is wrong with 'The Dead' is not a lack of talent in the author or the expression of an attitude to war which – in the light of history – seems unacceptably idealistic; but, rather, an attitude to what poetry is and ought to be which does not stand up to the demands being made of it by the human situation. I find it difficult to decide whether it is the point of view of the poet or his use of language that is at the root of the poem's unsatisfactoriness, because the two seem to me inextricably inter-twined. Some readers will want to say that 'The Dead' is insufficiently sincere, and that is one way of putting it, but one fraught with problems for it too easily implies that the poet does not 'really' mean what he says: whereas the trouble seems to me to lie in the situation rather than the poet's psyche. You might say that nothing up till then had happened to Rupert Brooke, as man or poet, to prepare him adequately to meet the challenge of the war and what it implied.

1.23   ■   What, then, are the 'new' elements in 'Dulce et Decorum Est' which distinguish it from the sort of poetry English readers before the First World War were most used to?

Discussion

1.24   *Subject matter*   It would not be true to say that nineteenth-century poets never wrote about war (remember 'The Charge of the Light Brigade') or that they only chose 'poetic' subjects for their poetry (think of Crabbe or Clough or Kipling). Yet there can be no doubt that a subject like a gas attack was not what most poetry readers associated with the idea of poetry. There is the implication in Owen's poetry that *anything* can be the subject of poetry and though many poets at many periods would have found nothing to object to in this implication it was certainly felt by a great many readers of his time to be something new.

1.25   *Commitment*   This is a 'committed' poem in the sense that the poet is in no way neutral about his subject matter and its implications. Now this certainly was not something new in poetry. *Most* of the Victorian poets moralized in their poetry. 'The Charge of the Light Brigade' is not a neutral poem, neither is Kipling's 'If', or, for that matter, Brooke's 'The Dead'. So it looks as though the commitment behind 'Dulce et Decorum Est', its 'propaganda' element (in the sense of deliberately trying to change the reader's attitudes), is not one of the new things about it. One might of course argue that the important thing about Owen's commitment, as opposed to Tennyson's or Kipling's or Brooke's, is that it is anti-establishment; it is a 'protest poem'. That is true and it was no doubt shocking (and in that sense novel) to conservative persons who read it and did not think that sort of thing ought to be said (even if it were true); but of course Owen was not the first poet – even among the widely-accepted ones – to write poetry of protest. Think of Shelley, Hood, Wilde. Indignation has often been a driving force of poetry. But again, it is not simply a matter of indignation or commitment in the abstract. Brooke's commitment to British nationalism was certainly strong: but was it, as a commitment, adequate to the situation he, and the British people as a whole, now had to face? Isn't there, behind the breakdown of a certain rhetoric, the breakup of a social order?

1.26 *Style* This is the crux of the question and more important than what I have rather uneasily called 'subject matter', for the subject matter of the poem – except in a very generalized and not very significant way – *is* the style. Said differently it would be a different poem. And how 'new' is the style?

1.27 Well, partly it depends what you compare it with. If you think of, say, Clough or Hopkins (whose work, though already written, Owen cannot have known), the contrast is not as great as all that. For example, Arthur Hugh Clough's 'Amours de Voyage' (published 1849)

> *Dulce* it is, and *decorum*, no doubt, for the country to fall, – to
> Offer one's blood an oblation to Freedom, and die for the Cause; yet
> Still, individual culture is also something, and no man
> Finds quite distinct the assurance that he of all others is called on,
> Or would be justified even, in taking away from the world that
> Precious creature, himself . . .

or, from Hopkins's 'Tom's Garland: upon the Unemployed' (written 1887, published 1918)

> Tom – garlanded with squat and surly steel
> Tom; then Tom's fallowbootfellow piles pick
> By him and rips out rockfire homeforth – sturdy Dick;
> Tom Heart-at-ease, Tom Navvy: he is all for his meal
> Sure, 's bed now. Low be it: lustily he his low lot (feel
> That ne'er need hunger, Tom; Tom seldom sick,
> Seldomer heartsore; that treads through, prickproof, thick
> Thousands of thorns, thoughts) swings though . . .

(Compare in particular, Hopkins's 'prickproof' with Owen's 'blood-shod'.)

That is also true of some of Hardy and even Browning, though he would not have gone as far as Owen. On the other hand, if you bear in mind neo-Romantic poetry in general or the Georgians, or Rupert Brooke's sonnet, there *is* a striking contrast.

1.28 It comes out partly in the rejection of the 'poetic' in the more 'beautiful' sense: one can scarcely imagine Tennyson or even Matthew Arnold describing this as a 'beautiful' poem. It also has something to do with the 'dramatic' nature of the poem, which again is partly why there is a certain link with Browning who also wrote dramatic monologues. Part of the sense of urgency Owen's poem evokes comes from plunging us into a dramatic situation in which people are on the move. It is not a contemplative poem, though in the end it makes you think. The language is not really colloquial (compare Kipling's poems about soldiers) but it is dramatic and this is true not only of the more descriptive bits of action, but of some of the most striking and lingering phrases: 'coughing like hags', 'blood-shod', 'His hanging face, like a devil's sick of sin'. The moral compassion embedded in the poem emerges from these images. It is only in the last few lines that Owen permits himself in such words as 'innocent', 'children' and 'ardent' the preacher's habit of 'pointing' the drama for his purposes: but until the use of the word 'lie' in his punch line he is careful not to step outside the dramatic framework he has created. A line like 'you too could pace/Behind the wagon that we flung him in', has nothing outwardly 'dramatic' (in the newspaper sense) about it but it tells 'you' (i.e. the 'friend' who is in fact an audience) all you need to know in dramatic terms. The tension between the objective, dramatic scene he presents and his own indignation which especially fills his adjectives seems to be one of the recurrent characteristics of Owen's style.

1.29　In one sense none of this is very new: many poets have used such means of expression. And yet both in his choice of language (in the more detailed sense) and in the nature of his relationship to his subject matter there is, I would like to argue, a significant 'newness', in the sense that one can say, here is something that is not just a new individual note (such as every good poet, simply because he is not someone else, has) but something that amounts to a significant development in poetic style. You can isolate it in the 'realism' of Owen's language, in the dissonances which replace rhymes and in what is best described perhaps as a sombre wit which counteracts and at best controls the intensity of direct personal emotion behind his poems.

1.30　A good deal of Owen's poetry seems to me to be 'new' without necessarily being 'modernist'. We will take 'Futility' as an example.

> *Futility*
>
> Move him into the sun –
> Gently its touch awoke him once,
> At home, whispering of fields unsown.
> Always it woke him, even in France,
> Until this morning and this snow.
> If anything might rouse him now
> The kind old sun will know.
>
> Think how it wakes the seeds, –
> Woke, once, the clays of a cold star.
> Are limbs, so dear-achieved, are sides,
> Full-nerved – still warm – too hard to stir?
> Was it for this the clay grew tall?
> – O what made fatuous sunbeams toil
> To break earth's sleep at all?

1.31　■　As you read and get to know this poem begin thinking about the questions:

a　What gives it its special quality as a poem?

b　In what ways, if any, could it be called a 'modernist' poem?

Discussion

1.32　a　Its poetic quality: some thoughts of mine to compare with yours.

1.33　The first line is an order: in other circumstances it might be a cruel one: here it becomes less of a command, more of an expression of common humanity with each reading. With the word 'kind' applied to the sun in the seventh line the basic contrast on which the poem is built becomes clear: on the one hand the sun, warmth, awakening, growth, touch, friendliness, normality, life; on the other the dead cold soldier. The moving of the corpse into the sun is the only gesture of affirmation which the men in the poem can make: it can do no good to him but it asserts *their* humanity.

1.34 The second part of the sonnet begins with the word 'think', balancing (but not just formally) the word 'move'. This part of the poem is about thoughts, implications: it explores the meaning of the gesture – spontaneous almost, futile in a way – the first part has revealed. Notice how the two parts are linked: by the sun, by the fields, by the clay, by the seeds. Life is seen with total concreteness, not mystically, but as the living process, arising out of the nature of the universe,[1] growing in complexity, generated by and generating warmth, fellow feeling, potentiality.

1.35 The death of the soldier is queried, therefore, in the light of the most basic possible issues: 'Was it for this the clay grew tall?' The linking of 'fatuous' with sunbeams (associated, notice, with toil or energy not with prettiness) expresses all the poet needs to say in criticism of what man has made of man.

1.36 The 'futility' of the title may at first give a sense of some sort of pettiness or narrowness. But what strikes me most about this poem when I try to sum up its impact is that I cannot avoid making the central word humanity. It is a poem about the human condition, not conceived metaphysically as some more or less unchanging state, but in the sense of a betrayal of humanity and nature, a gross perversion of the potentiality of what human development could mean.

1.37 b Would you call it a 'modernist' poem?

1.38 Not at all an easy question. 'Modernist' (as Nick Furbank has warned us) is so difficult to define and not always used consistently. If poems like Yeats's 'Among School-children' or 'On a Political Prisoner' are to be called 'modernist', then I can see no good reason for excluding 'Futility' from the category.

1.39 Yet there are reasons for drawing back. Owen's poem is certainly not one which involves any very sharp break with nineteenth-century tradition. No one brought up on Romantic poetry would be likely to find it very difficult. A reader who could cope with Matthew Arnold's 'Dover Beach' would not find in coming upon 'Futility' (as opposed to, say, Eliot's 'Prufrock') that he had entered a new poetic world.

1.40 Compared with most nineteenth-century poetry, though, there is a rather unusual mixture of austerity and complexity (emerging perhaps in the Hopkins-like 'dear-achieved', in the uncompromising 'fatuous', and also, I think, in the shorthand 'even in France'): though you get this in Hardy's poetry too.

1.41 I cannot help feeling that an important characteristic that separates Owen's poem from the poetry we generally think of as 'modernist' is the absence of a mediating factor (some sort of self-conscious 'art' or 'convention') between the poet and his audience. Owen speaks with a traditional (Romantic?) direct simplicity to his reader as man to man. Perhaps this is what Day Lewis had in mind when he said of this poem that 'poetical truth (became) here, as in almost all his poems, the servant of common honesty.'

1.42 Wilfred Owen's affinity with Keats is well known. It comes out in detailed as well as more general ways in his poetry. Generally, what happens is that something of Keats' is transmogrified in Owen.

> O Sorrow,
> Why dost borrow
> The natural hue of health, from vermeil lips?[2]

becomes

> Red lips are not so red
> As the stained stones kissed by the English dead

[1] I am reminded of a line of Wallace Stevens: 'We live in an old chaos of the sun.'
[2] Keats, 'The Indian Woman's Song' from 'Endymion' Book IV *Poetical Works*.

Behind the mysterious poem 'Strange Meeting' lies, somewhere not altogether easy to identify, Keats' 'Fall of Hyperion'.

1.43　You can see how Keats hangs around Owen in the first stanza of the poem 'Greater Love' which I have just mentioned.

> Red lips are not so red
>   As the stained stones kissed by the English dead.
> Kindness of wooed and wooer
> Seems shame to their love pure.
> O Love, your eyes lose lure
>   When I behold eyes blinded in my stead.

It is not just the echoes from 'The Indian Woman's Song': the whole use of language and rhyme, the whole conception of what poetry most basically *is* remains Keatsian. 'Greater Love' is a war poem. Owen is facing brutalities of a sort Keats, for all his unhappiness and courage, never had to face. And he is also facing, as the middle-class Romantic poets never quite had to face, the nature of his relationship to 'others', who *share* his fate. What comes out, at that stage of his experience, is a mixture of Romantic poetry and the experience of the trenches: Keats brought up to date you might say. Or again, you might prefer to say an uneasy alliance between what Keats called poesy and a different sort of reality.

1.44　Owen had to fight against Keats. He knew very well that a poet who had lived a century earlier and in a very different world could only half help him. And it is only a slight exaggeration to say that Owen, in order to fulfil not only himself but Keats too, knew he had to purge his style of a good deal of Keatsian rhetoric. In this respect it is fair to draw a parallel between Owen and Yeats,[3] who also, in Pound's words, had been forced to 'strip English poetry of its perdamnable rhetoric'.[4]

1.45　The difference between Yeats' path to a more 'modern' poetry and Owen's lies partly, I think, in the differences between the nature of the Irish liberation struggle with which Yeats more than half identified, and that of the First World War which Owen came to feel was the enemy of all he wanted; but also partly with the two poets' attitude to art. For Yeats, art was always the thing: while Owen, with his love-hate relationship with Keats, had a much more ambivalent attitude.

1.46　■　At this point it is necessary to quote the famous Preface Owen wrote for his own poems:

> This book is not about heroes. English Poetry is not yet fit to speak of them.
>
> Nor is it about deeds, or lands, nor anything about glory, honour, might, majesty, dominion, or power, except War.
>
> Above all I am not concerned with Poetry.
>
> My subject is War, and the pity of War.
>
> The Poetry is in the pity.

---

[3]One of Owen's poems '(S.I.W.)' begins with a quotation from Yeats of some significance

> I will to the King,
> And offer him consolation in his trouble,
> For that man there has set his teeth to die,
> And being one that hates obedience,
> Discipline, and orderliness of life,
> I cannot mourn him.

[4]Yeats himself said (in a broadcast in 1936) 'My generation, because it disliked Victorian rhetorical moral fervour, came to dislike all rhetoric.' (Yeats *Selected Criticism*, p 244.)

Yet these elegies are to this generation in no sense consolatory. They may be to the next. All a poet can do today is warn. That is why the true Poets must be truthful. (Owen, *Poems*.)

It is worth reading these sentences several times to allow the thoughts Owen is expressing to get their full force. How do they compare, would you say, with the manifestoes and theories of the Imagists and other 'modernist' poets referred to in the earlier part of this unit? Do you find a contrast between Owen's attitude to poetry and those of the 'modernists'?

Discussion

1.47 Certainly it is hard to imagine any of the 'modernists' saying 'Above all I am not concerned with Poetry.' They were supremely concerned with poetry. But then so, after all, in his way was Wilfred Owen: otherwise he would not have felt so passionately about it. It is true that the phrase 'The Poetry is in the pity' seems to go strongly against the sort of thing Pound, Eliot and the 'modernists' believed. They thought that the way out of the mess was through a concentration on poetry itself, through 'purging' and 'purifying' it, through admitting everything – all experience and, especially, all intelligence and all culture to it. They were sceptical about basing poetry on a too direct and personal emotion. But then, of course, Owen too is saying that the *object* (war) rather than the *subject* (the poet) is the important thing. And when he says 'Above all I am not concerned with Poetry' isn't he perhaps stressing that he is not concerned with poetry as it *has been* thought of? It seems to me at least arguable that Owen, whose concern with poetry is manifest, is warning against an aestheticism which has too limited a view of beauty, rather than against the poet's being conscious that his job is to produce art. It is *through* poetry that Owen's poet must warn. The 'modernists', especially if one includes Yeats, would not have disagreed with that.

1.48 Nevertheless there *is* an important contrast between Owen's statements and 'modernist' practice. What Owen is arguing for includes something which later writers have called 'commitment'.[5] And the sort of commitment Owen is indicating in his Preface is significantly different from, say, Eliot's commitment to Christianity or 'tradition' or even Yeats' relation to the Irish national movement. One of its main features is the poet's sense of 'sharing' the experience of many others. Now it is true that Owen's attitude to the war as it emerges from his poetry is not without some of the more orthodox 'establishment' virtues involving such principles as 'leadership', 'responsibility', 'setting an example', looking after your men (or horses) before yourself. Owen was an officer, and a highly responsible one. But the war also made him a sharer in a fuller sense than the officer's code implies. I think this comes out in the poem 'Futility' already discussed.

1.49 Please read that poem again, if you do not quite remember it.

1.50 Do you find anything 'superior' about it? Any evidence that Owen, either as officer or artist, is separating himself from his subject? Personally, I find no such separation: the humanity evoked by the short poem seems to me single and to include, in complete equality, the dead boy, the poet and the reader. The first line, which *might* be the order of an officer to his men and carry that degree of dissociation from them, is in fact an order no officer would ever give: it is the *poet* speaking and the imperative

[5] I shall discuss it more fully in Units 21–22.

is addressed to the reader as much as to the soldiers who carry the dead man. There is a sense in which 'Move him into the sun' corresponds with Owen's determination, shared with his friend Sassoon, to bring the whole truth about the war into the open.

1.51 Let us take another, bigger, poem of Owen's, the one called 'Insensibility'

I

Happy are men who yet before they are killed
Can let their veins run cold.
Whom no compassion fleers
Or makes their feet
Sore on the alleys cobbled with their brothers.
The front line withers,
But they are troops who fade, not flowers
For poets' tearful fooling:
Men, gaps for filling:
Losses who might have fought
Longer; but no one bothers.

II

And some cease feeling
Even themselves or for themselves.
Dullness best solves
The tease and doubt of shelling,
And Chance's strange arithmetic
Comes simpler than the reckoning of their shilling.
They keep no check on armies' decimation.

III

Happy are these who lose imagination:
They have enough to carry with ammunition.
Their spirit drags no pack,
Their old wounds save with cold can not more ache.
Having seen all things red,
Their eyes are rid
Of the hurt of the colour of blood for ever.
And terror's first constriction over,
Their hearts remain small-drawn.
Their senses in some scorching cautery of battle
Now long since ironed,
Can laugh among the dying, unconcerned.

IV

Happy the soldier home, with not a notion
How somewhere, every dawn, some men attack,
And many sighs are drained.
Happy the lad whose mind was never trained:
His days are worth forgetting more than not.
He sings along the march
Which we march taciturn, because of dusk,
The long, forlorn, relentless trend
From larger day to huger night.

V

We wise, who with a thought besmirch
Blood over all our soul,
How should we see our task
But through his blunt and lashless eyes?
Alive, he is not vital overmuch;
Dying, not mortal overmuch;
Nor sad, nor proud,
Nor curious at all.
He cannot tell
Old men's placidity from his.

VI

But cursed are dullards whom no cannon stuns,
That they should be as stones;
Wretched are they, and mean
With paucity that never was simplicity.
By choice they made themselves immune
To pity and whatever moans in man
Before the last sea and the hapless stars;
Whatever mourns when many leave these shores;
Whatever shares
The eternal reciprocity of tears.

1.52   The poem is not difficult, line by line, though its implications are not always immediately clear. What is difficult at first is to establish the precise tone – the tone that makes the first two lines both shocking and plausible; for though we realize that 'happy' must contain some sort of irony we are not sure what this implies. Lines six to eleven are so cryptic, so emptied of all conventional 'poetic' paraphernalia, that we cannot be sure where the poet is leading us. Is he advocating insensibility as the only way of coping with a situation in which cynicism has replaced even minimal humanity? Is the 'poets' tearful fooling' evoked simply to indicate the futility of writing about flowers when the world is the way it is?

1.53   In the second and third sections the ambiguity is extended. Insensibility is seen as a deliberate tactic, a sort of drug, a way of meeting the intolerable. To lose imagination is one more step in necessary self-defence. To persuade men to laugh among the dying, unconcerned, is the final price the war exacts.

1.54   ■ Then in the fourth section comes a change, not yet in the movement of the poem (unless in the deliberately problematic line 'His days are worth forgetting more than not') but in its 'argument'. A new word creeps in, hitherto absent. Which word am I referring to?

Discussion

1.55   The word 'we'. Up to now the poem has been about 'them'. But from now on it has a new complexity: what is to be the relationship between 'us' and 'them'?

1.56   At first perhaps (and in section five) the introduction of 'we' may seem to extend and deepen the prevailing irony of the poem. 'We wise' looks like being half-ironical. ('We' emerge as a sort of Hamlet-figure for whom 'thought' is what distinguishes us from 'them' yet at the same time makes life intolerable.) It is hard to tell which attitude the poet is sympathetic to. There is force to the argument

> How should we see our task
> But through his blunt and lashless eyes?

Yet the words 'blunt' and 'lashless' are deeply ambiguous. 'Blunt' can mean honest but also not sharp enough. 'Lashless' may mean that the lashes have been burned off by explosion or fire: but it also conveys 'animal' rather than 'human'. Then the next line takes this idea further ('not vital overmuch' – ambiguous again in that it links with the earlier 'gaps for filling', the individual soldier is not really 'vital' to those who plan the war): and the following one ('Dying not mortal overmuch') takes the doubt about his humanity even further.

■ How is the poem to be resolved? How do you take the last section of the poem? Who are the dullards who are cursed?

Discussion

1.57 I used to think the 'dullards' of section six were distinguishable from the lads whose minds were never trained and who had drugged themselves by insensibility. It is possible to read the poem as though the people referred to at the end (the dullards) are those 'at home' in contrast to those facing the cannon in the trenches and I once read it that way. In other words I used to read the poem as though it were distinguishing between those who *deliberately* turned themselves into brutes (and who were therefore cursed) and those who did so unconsciously and who therefore deserved compassion. I now think such a reading is wrong, and the dullards of section six include those who have in the earlier reaches of the poem been characterized as 'happy'.

1.58 What Owen is surely asserting in these final lines is that there is a *choice* involved in the situation – awful as it is – that he is describing. To make a division between the sensitive and the insensitive on any other basis is to deny one's common humanity, to agree that some people are not vital, or even mortal, overmuch. The assertion of common humanity culminating in the phrase

> Whatever shares
> The eternal reciprocity of tears

seems to me to cast its meaning back over the whole poem, illuminating the nature of the struggle going on within the poet's being to resolve the contradiction between his compassion for those who (to use a phrase of Sassoon's) drug themselves with lies and his conviction that to do so is to betray something that must not be betrayed: he is trying to fill, if you like, the gap between 'them' and 'us'.

1.59 I have stressed this sense of sharing a common humanity, of filling a gap, in Owen's poetry because it seems to me to involve more than subject matter and to say something about other gaps – between poetry and 'life', between the poet and his audience – relevant to a general consideration of twentieth-century poetry.

1.60 Where Owen joins forces with the 'modernists' is in his attempt, forced on him by the experience of the war, to bring poetry into a closer, more comprehensive and more responsible relationship with life itself, to purge poetry not just of a false rhetoric but of a bogus 'position', abstracted from the flow of common human experience. He shared with Pound and Yeats and Eliot the sense that neo-Romantic poetry was not a sufficiently *serious* response to the situation poets found themselves in.

1.61 Yet in so far as 'modernist' poetry is, or says it is, as Nick Furbank puts it, not 'about' anything at all, but is, rather, 'self-sufficient' and 'self-justifying', there is clearly a difference of emphasis between this and Owen's insistence that his poetry is 'about' war. Nick Furbank underlines this when he says 'it sometimes seems that all a modernist poet can do, having written one poem, is to write another different one', a sentence which echoes (but reverses) Owen's own phrase 'All a poet can do today is warn.'

1.62 It can be argued, as I have already suggested, that the contrast here is more apparent than real, that no poem is really 'self-sufficient' and that Owen is more interested in 'poetry' and less in 'pity' than he claims. It can also be argued that the 'modernists' were more interested in 'warning' than their 'purer' statements about poetic practice might suggest. Pound, later in life, became 'committed' – to fascism; Eliot to Anglican Christianity. So one should be careful not to make intractable distinction between 'modernist' and 'non-modernist' poetry.

1.63 ■ Is the distinction between Owen and Pound more fruitfully thought of, perhaps, in terms of the poet's relationship to the outside reality, social and historical, about which he is writing? Nick Furbank quotes the impressive passage from Pound's 'Mauberley' about the First World War (para. 9.6). Please turn back and read it again. You will be struck, I think, by the way in which experience and attitudes encompassed in the Rupert Brooke and Wilfred Owen poems I have been discussing are included and given a new sort of unity in Pound's poem. How would you compare the Pound, *as poetry*, with Owen's 'Insensibility'?

Discussion

1.64 I think I would stress the relative impersonality or even objectivity of Pound's piece – not that Pound's personal feelings and quirks do not inform it – in the sense that in 'Mauberley' the poet is more distant and detached from what he is writing about. In one sense, that is, because in another Pound is clearly not 'detached' at all. The image 'an old bitch gone in the teeth' to describe the society for which the war was fought shows that. It is not a phrase Owen would have used: I think he would have considered it too *general*, a bit facile even.

1.65 It is tempting to hitch on to the word 'abstraction' in any attempt to define what was new in the poetry of the 'modernists'. 'Go in fear of abstraction' wrote Pound and the whole shift from the logic of conceptual thought to the logic of imagery in 'modernist' poetry is clearly pretty basic. And if you turn back to our earlier comparison between the Rupert Brooke sonnet and Owen's 'Dulce et Decorum Est' you will see its relevance. The real trouble with Brooke's sonnet, and what makes it, half a century later, almost embarrassing compared with Owen's poem, is Brooke's reliance on abstract nouns which simply do not stand up to the significance they are supposed to have. Owen, in contrast, is specific, particular, concrete. His own experience of the lies of the war-propagandists taught him to 'go in fear of abstractions'. When he uses an abstract noun, like futility or insensibility, he uses it not as an easy short cut but as a base for reconnaissance and manoeuvre, treading cagily, very much aware of the minefields around him.

1.66 It is true that all poets should go in fear of abstractions, particularly at a time of crisis when words, like bombs, are apt to explode in their hands. Pound's advice was relevant, not just to a poet like Yeats who took it up very seriously, but to his generation. Yet it is also true that 'modernist' and *symboliste* poets themselves use abstractions. Think of the work a word like 'incarnation' does in Eliot's later poetry, for example, from the final section of 'The Dry Salvages'.

> . . . These are only hints and guesses,
> Hints followed by guesses; and the rest
> Is prayer, observance, discipline, thought and action.
> The hint half guessed, the gift half understood, is Incarnation.

> Here the impossible union
> Of spheres of existence is actual,
> Here the past and future
> Are conquered, and reconciled,
> Where action were otherwise movement
> Of that which is only moved
> And has in it no source of movement –
> Driven by daemonic, chthonic
> Powers. And right action is freedom
> From past and future also . . .

1.67   It occurs to me that one way of describing what poets were seeking in the first twenty years of the present century is to say they felt the need of a new culture. Not so much new ideas or values or forms or styles or words (though these were all, obviously, of high importance and occupied most of their time) as a cultural framework within which they could move with reasonable freedom and which could sustain them in their battle to achieve expression. Pound, Eliot, Yeats all invented a 'tradition' which suited their needs. The tradition Wilfred Owen worked in was, essentially, the tradition of English Romanticism, which the 'modernists' rejected. Behind his poems and his Preface lurk Keats and Wordsworth. I think the word 'democracy' is also relevant. In a deep sense which involves the whole level of communication between poet and audience, Owen's poetry is more democratic than that of the 'modernists'.

Perhaps I should develop those last thoughts a little.

1.68   When I bring Romanticism (partly via Keats) into the argument it is not 'style' or 'literary history' in the narrower sense I have in mind. The essential thing about the English Romantic poets of the turn of the eighteenth–nineteenth centuries (veterans of A202 *The Age of Revolutions*[6] will perhaps be at an advantage here) is that they rejected not just a vocabulary but a whole conception of life and values which they associated with a limited, because essentially aristocratic, society. Wordsworth called on poets to re-examine the 'language of men' in the light of a new way of looking at (more) men (and women) which the social developments of his time, an age of revolutions, implied and demanded. Shelley in *The Defence of Poetry* and in his more radical poems expressed a view of poetry which combined an emphasis on what is 'new' ('hitherto unapprehended combinations of thought and feeling') with what is, in the broadest sense of the term 'democratic' (linking concepts of 'man' or 'humanity' with a pervading sense of the possibility of a universal liberty, equality, fraternity). One of the driving forces of Romanticism was a profound desire on the part of poets to 'unite' with the forces of human liberation released by the French Revolution. The last movement of Beethoven's Choral Symphony and the second act of *Fidelio* are supreme expressions of this impulse and this is what, above all, distinguishes them from the more aristocratic art of Mozart, despite the latter's lack of complacency about the pre-revolutionary society.

1.69   Romanticism of course took many forms. Romantic artists, as Nick Furbank points out, often felt themselves to be very isolated and later Romantic art tended to become very inward-turned and even neurotic – the very opposite of Beethoven's celebration of freedom and brotherhood or Shelley's words to the men of England:

> Rise like lions after slumber
> In unvanquishable number –
> Shake your chains to earth like dew
> Which in sleep had fallen on you –
> Ye are many – they are few.

[6]The Open University (1972) A202 *The Age of Revolutions*, The Open University Press.

For Shelley 'they' are the rulers, the few are the enemy; while 'you', the many, are the people to unite with (though it is not only the construction of his poem, I think, that makes him say 'ye' rather than 'we'). My point is that the Romantic poets and even their later, less convinced Victorian followers, basically wanted to *unite* with other people, to extend, rather than limit the bounds of fellow-feeling and a unified human consciousness. When they found they could not do this (because what the French Revolution ushered in was a society very different from what Wordsworth and Shelley and Blake had hoped for) they may have become neurotic but they still accepted, at bottom, that it would have been better not to live in a condition of alienation; hence the odd and sometimes guilt-ridden forms their alienation took, as well as the appeal that idealistic and phoney forms of 'unity' ('national' unity included) often had for them. I am thinking of Tennyson's hero in *Maud* working himself up into a state in which the Crimean War seems the solution to all personal and public dilemmas, of Browning whipping himself up to an all-embracing (but not very well-founded) optimism, of Kipling taking on the white man's burden, and – if it comes to that – Rupert Brooke pouring out all those high-minded sentiments about honour, nobleness, etc. as a response to the 1914 war.

1.70 Romanticism, I am suggesting, came out of that stage of the bourgeois-democratic revolution which started in Europe in 1789 and as a response and contribution to what happened in Europe in the nineteenth century it embodied all the aspirations and weaknesses, all the achievements and illusions, the successes and failures, in a word the contradictory reality, of that revolution. In England it carried poetry irrevocably out of the Augustan world (which did not prevent a poet like Byron or Crabbe making excellent use of the Augustan achievement), and it is as impossible to 'reject' Romanticism as to 'reject' the French Revolution, or the emancipation of the slaves.

1.71 'Modernism' did however in an important sense reject, or try to reject, Romanticism. I am not just thinking of T. E. Hulme and his more extreme statements but of something much wider involved, for instance, in the whole critical theory of T. S. Eliot. The playing up of the metaphysical poets at the expense of the Romantics, the shabby treatment of Romantic critics in Eliot's *The Use of Poetry and the Use of Criticism* : these are examples of what I am pointing to.[7] And of course the 'modernists' *had to* reject Romanticism: to do so was a part – and probably a necessary one – of their need to develop an alternative way of looking at the world with enough energy and élan to carry them through to the sort of expression they were seeking. I agree with Nick Furbank that the 'modernists' did manage to find new ways of coping with that alienation which the late Romantic artists had tended to wallow in. There are good reasons for preferring the music of Stravinsky to that of Strauss or Mahler.

1.72 But there was a cost and it is well indicated if you compare Pound's passage on the First World War in 'Mauberley' with Wilfred Owen's or Siegfried Sassoon's war poetry. Isn't there something rather objectionably 'superior' and a shade dishonest about the Pound passage? And isn't the poetic stance behind the modernists' poetry (articulated in Eliot's important essay 'Tradition and the Individual Talent', reprinted in the Course Reader) significantly linked with the authoritarian politics of Pound and Hulme, Eliot and Yeats? Again, we shall be coming back to such questions later in the course and perhaps the question should be postponed.

1.73 I am not arguing of course that the 'modernists' were bad poets because of their authoritarian politics, nor wanting to lump them all together anyway. (Yeats is a very complex case and both his Irish national consciousness and his respect for the Romantics and Blake are important.) It is certainly arguable that the later expressions of Romantic art towards the end of the nineteenth century – Swinburne's poetry for instance – were getting nowhere very satisfactory and that the new

[7]Eliot's criticism will be discussed in Unit 9.

directions which a Hardy on the one hand or a Kipling on the other explored *within* the Romantic tradition were insufficiently radical. I am emphatically not arguing against 'modernism'. But I think there is a danger in tending to assume, as most of us do nowadays, that the 'modernist' developments were the essential answers to the questions and dilemmas of artists working at the turn of the nineteenth–twentieth centuries. Are we quite sure that a line or tradition that includes Clough, Hopkins (some might complain about putting him there but I would argue that he works, though with radical innovations, within the Romantic tradition), Hardy and Owen is really less 'central' than one that emerges from an emphasis on the *Symbolistes* and Imagists, Pound and Eliot (I again leave out Yeats because he straddles the two lines of development)? I ask the question not to try to denigrate the work of the 'modernists' but to avoid the implication that 'modernism' is to be seen as necessarily 'the answer' as far as a twentieth-century poetic goes.

1.74 You may complain that this sort of talk about 'lines' and 'traditions' and 'isms' is not really much to the point anyway and can easily become a rather intellectually snobbish alternative to talking about actual poems and their particular unique essence. What the hell does it matter whether Wilfred Owen belongs to a 'Romantic tradition' or not? Perhaps it would be salutary at this point to do a small exercise. If your response to that last indignant question is sympathetic (i.e. if you tend to feel impatient about 'traditions' and 'isms') try to formulate some of the reasons why some literary critics *do* feel such talk can be illuminating, and not purely as a rather narrow exercise of a 'literary history' sort. If, on the other hand, you are at home amidst such concepts as 'Romanticism', 'modernism', etc., try and state clearly the case *against* that particular approach and vocabulary.

1.75 We will come back to this general question of critical method at various later points in the course. I raise it in this form now because the very word 'modernism' challenges all kinds of responses and problems and an essay like Eliot's 'Tradition and the Individual Talent' may well present a helpful way in to some of the problems a consideration of 'modernist' poetry raises.

REFERENCES

Creighton, T. M. R. (ed.) (1975) *Poems of Thomas Hardy: A New Selection*, Macmillan (Set book.)

Eliot, T. S. (1964) *The Use of Poetry and the Use of Criticism*, Faber. (First published 1933.)

Empson, William (1940) *The Gathering Storm*, Faber.

Ginsberg, Allen (1956) *Howl*, City Light Books.

Hynes, Samuel (1967) *The Edwardian Turn of Mind*, Princeton University Press.

Joyce, James (1969) *Giacomo Joyce*, Faber.

Kermode, Frank (1957) *Romantic Image*, Routledge.

Lawrence, D. H. (1917) *Look! We Have Come Through!*: (1918) *New Poems*: (1928) *Collected Poems*. Available in *Complete Poems*.

Lehmann, A. G. (1950) *The Symbolist Aesthetic in France, 1885–95*, Blackwell.

Lowell, Robert (1959) *Life Studies*, Faber.

Martin, Graham and Furbank, P. N. (eds.) (1975) *Twentieth Century Poetry: Critical Essays and Documents*, The Open University Press. (Course Reader.)

Owen, Wilfred (1960) (ed. Blunden) *Poems*, Chatto and Windus. (First published 1931.)

Pound, Ezra (1960) *Gaudier Brzeska: A Memoir*, Marvell Press. (First published 1916.)
Pound, Ezra (1975) *Ezra Pound: Selected Poems 1908–1959*, Faber. (Set book.)
Press, John (1969) *A Map of Modern English Verse*, Oxford University Press. (Set book.)
Silkin, Jon (1972) *Out of Battle*, Oxford University Press.
Yeats, W. B. (1918) 'Per Amica Silentia Lunae', reprinted (1962) in *Mythologies*, Macmillan.
Yeats, W. B. (1950) *Collected Poems of W. B. Yeats*, Macmillan. (Set bo

ACKNOWLEDGEMENTS

Grateful acknowledgement is made to the copyright holders for the following:

HILDA DOOLITTLE, 'Heat' and 'Oread' from *Selected Poems of H. D.* Copyright 1957 by Norman Holmes Pearson. Reprinted by permission of New Directions Publishing Corp. Inc. for Norman Holmes Pearson.

T. S. ELIOT, 'The Waste Land', 'La Figlia che Piange' and 'Hysteria' from *Collected Poems 1909–1962*. Reprinted by permission of Faber and Faber and Harcourt Brace Jovanovich, Inc; copyright 1963, 1964, by T. S. Eliot.

T. E. HULME, 'Autumn' from Ezra Pound's *Collected Shorter Poems*. Reprinted by permission of Faber and Faber and New Directions Publishing Corp. Inc.

JAMES JOYCE, pp 1–3 from *Giacomo Joyce*. Reprinted by permission of Faber and Faber and The Viking Press.

MALLARMÉ, 'Victoriously fled' from *Poems of Mallarmé* translated by Roger Fry. Reprinted by permission of Mrs Pamela Diamand and Chatto and Windus.

MALLARMÉ, 'Winter Shivering' from *Poetry of Mallarmé* translated by Anthony Hartley. Reprinted by permission of Penguin Books Ltd.

EZRA POUND, 'Fan piece for her Imperial Lord', 'Hugh Selwyn Mauberley' section IV Part 1, 'April' and 'Gentildonna' from *Collected Shorter Poems*. Reprinted by permission of Faber and Faber and New Directions Publishing Corp. Inc.

WALLACE STEVENS, 'Banal Sojourn' from *Collected Poems*. Reprinted by permission of Faber and Faber and Random House, Inc.

DYLAN THOMAS, 'Because the pleasure-bird whistles' from *Collected Poems*. Reprinted by permission of J. M. Dent and Sons Ltd, the Trustees for the copyright of the late Dylan Thomas and New Directions Publishing Corp. Inc.

EDWARD THOMAS, 'October' from *Collected Poems by Edward Thomas*. Reprinted by permission of Mrs Myfanwy Thomas and Faber and Faber.

WILLIAM CARLOS WILLIAMS, 'Poem' from *Collected Earlier Poems*. Reprinted by permission of Laurence Pollinger Ltd, and New Directions Publishing Corp. Inc. Copyright 1938.

W. B. YEATS, 'The Song of the Happy Shepherd', 'The Indian to His Love', 'Among Schoolchildren', 'Who goes with Fergus', 'Adam's Curse' and 'The Magi' from *Collected Poems*. Reprinted by permission of M. B. Yeats, Miss Anne Yeats, Macmillan of London and Basingstoke, Macmillan Co. of Canada and Macmillan Publishing Co. Inc.

W. B. YEATS, 'An Indian Song' from *The Variorum Edition of the Poems of W. B. Yeats*. Reprinted by permission of M. B. Yeats, Miss Anne Yeats, and Macmillan of London and Basingstoke and Macmillan Publishing Co. Inc.